# WOODEN
# DINKY TOYS

### SIMPLE TECHNIQUES & COMPLETE PLANS
### TO BUILD 18 TINY CLASSICS

Publisher: Paul McGahren
Editorial Director: Matthew Teague
Editor: Kerri Grzybicki
Designer: Lindsay Hess
Layout Designer: Jodie Delohery
Illustrator: Carolyn Mosher
Indexer: Jay Kreider

Spring House Press
P.O. Box 239
Whites Creek, TN 37189

ISBN: 978-1-940611-82-2 (print)

Library of Congress Control Number: 2019936682

Printed in The United States of America
10 9 8 7 6 5 4 3 2 1

Note: The following list contains names that may be used in *Wooden Dinky Toys* and may be registered with the United States Copyright Office: Batmobile; Bell (UH-1); Bigfoot 4x4; Chance Vought (F4U Corsair); Corgi; de Havilland Canada (Beaver); Dinky Toys; F-16; Ferrari; Ford (Deuce Coupe); Hot Wheels; James Bond; Lesney; Maserati; Matchbox; Mattel; Meccano; Northern Nightmare; P-51 Mustang; Simba Dickie Group (Majorette); Thunderbirds; Tomy (Ertl); TootsieToys; and United States Coast Guard.

The information in this book is given in good faith; however, no warranty is given, nor are results guaranteed. Woodworking is inherently dangerous. Your safety is your responsibility. Neither Spring House Press nor the authors assume any responsibility for any injuries or accidents.

To learn more about Spring House Press books, or to find a retailer near you, email info@springhousepress.com or visit us at www.springhousepress.com.

# WOODEN
# DINKY TOYS

## SIMPLE TECHNIQUES & COMPLETE PLANS
## TO BUILD 18 TINY CLASSICS

LES NEUFELD

SPRING HOUSE PRESS

# CONTENTS

## LAND

24

**Pickup Truck**
26

**Fifth-Wheel Flat Deck Trailer**
32

**Fifth-Wheel RV Trailer**
39

**Cab-Over Truck**
47

**Flat Deck Trailer for Cab-Over Truck**
54

**Deuce Coupe**
59

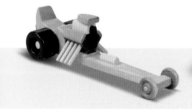

**Dragster**
64

**Monster Trucks x 3**
76

**School Bus**
87

**1930s Sprint Car**
94

# INTRODUCTION

**Generations of youngsters** have grown up playing with small die-cast metal toy cars, trucks, planes, boats, military vehicles, and spacecraft. Dinky, Corgi, Matchbox, Majorette, Ertl, and Hot Wheels have produced billions of these toys since the Dowst brothers began making TootsieToys in 1920s Chicago. New die-casting methods resulted in realistic, durable, and inexpensive toys.

I asked my son (now in his 20s) to dig out his die-cast toys for a photo. He happily did so. This photo shows about half of the toys he still had, and includes toys from 15 to 50 years old. Some show signs of much use, some are still like new. Most households probably have a similar or larger collection.

## BRIEF HISTORY

In the 1930s, Frank Hornby, inventor of Hornby trains and Meccano sets, began making Dinky Toys to accompany his train sets. "Dinky" was a Scottish word meaning "neat" or "small". Dinky toys quickly became hugely popular on their own. By 1938, Meccano was manufacturing 300 models of Dinky Toys, representing land, sea, and air travel. Before long, they were producing several million toys each week.

Ertl began making toys in Iowa in 1945, producing many farm equipment toys, as well as other toys. Ertl made die-cast toys for about 60 years.

The 1950s saw other companies (Lesney, Corgi) begin to make similar toys. These toys were based on popular vehicles of the day, as well as toys from movies such as Corgi's Batmobile and James Bond

Die-cast toys

**Wooden dinky toys**

cars. Matchbox toys were introduced by Lesney in the 1950s when the daughter of a co-owner was only allowed to bring toys to school if they were small enough to fit inside a matchbox. Lesney began producing small toys that were packaged in matchboxes. These little toys could be carried in a pocket, and dozens of them could be stored in a shoebox.

Mattel introduced the astonishingly successful Hot Wheels brand in 1968. These small die-cast toys included "tricked-out" toys of all types. In 2018, Mattel celebrated the manufacture of its four-billionth Hot Wheels toy. Mattel brands now include Corgi, Matchbox, and Dinky toys to go along with their original Hot Wheels line.

## POPULARITY

Today these small toys are more popular than ever. Not only do kids still love them, (apparently Mattel currently sells ten Hot Wheels toys every second), but many adults have extensive collections as well.

The small size of these toys is a big part of the appeal. The cars are typically only 2½ to 3 in. long.

The low cost of die-cast is another factor in their amazing popularity. Die-casting is an extremely fast and inexpensive way to mass-produce detailed toys and toy parts—once the reusable mold or "die" has been made. Even today, many new Hot Wheels diecast toys are on the store shelves for about $1.

The toys in this book have the same advantages. They are relatively quick to make: most can be made over a weekend and some can be finished in a day. The cost is very low because of the tiny amount of wood used. And, like the original toys, these can be carried around in a pocket or in a small box. A dozen of them can be lined up and played with on a window sill.

# MATERIALS & TOOLS

Here are the materials and tools you'll need to create the projects in this book.

- Tablesaw
- Scroll saw or bandsaw
- Push sticks
- Drill press or handheld drill with countersink, twist, Forstner, and hole cutting bits
- Disc sander or sanding board
- Clamps
- Square
- Compass
- Block plane
- Sandpaper in various grits
- Files
- Screwdrivers
- Spray finish of choice
- Wood glue (Titebond III or equivalent recommended)
- Masking tape
- Pencil
- Carbon paper
- Scissors

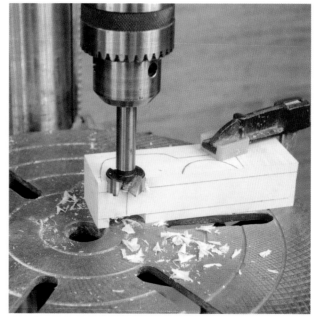

A drill press with a selection of bits, along with a variety of clamps, are a few of the tools you'll need for these projects.

You'll see that safety guards are sometimes raised in the step photographs to show the step clearly. Guards should be lowered when cutting.

# CHOOSING WOOD

## AVAILABILITY

Toys provide a good chance to use up the small off-cuts left over from other projects, or to use more exotic woods that you have not used due to high prices. The toys in this book could all be made from my local woods, like birch or box elder. The other woods shown were used only for a bit of variety and because I happened to have off-cuts available.

## COST

Many of the toys use so little wood that even an expensive wood is a viable choice, if you can find only a small amount. Most toys will use only a fraction of a board foot. The typical size, about 1 x 1 x 4 in., is only 1/36 of a board foot. Even at $20 a board foot, this will only set you back about 55 cents.

## FIGURE & GRAIN

I have found that my favorite beautifully figured, treasured pieces of wood make for particularly unattractive toys! The wonderful grain obscures the outlines of the toy and makes it look more like a nice piece of wood than a fun toy. So, I have learned to use close-grained wood, preferably with grain that is scarcely noticeable.

## DURABILITY

I also prefer woods that are hard and dent-resistant. Toys can often take a bit of a beating, and this helps them be longer wearing.

## COLOR

If possible, I choose wood that has a coloring appropriate to the toy, such as yellowheart for the school bus. I repeatedly used a couple of local woods, which for me was birch and box elder (also known as Manitoba maple or maple ash). Both those woods yield light-colored toys. I had scraps of purpleheart, bloodwood, padauk, and wenge, so used those as well for more brightly colored toys.

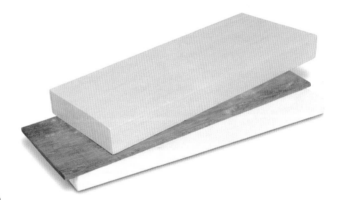

Close-grained wood with a mild grain works well for these toys.

# WHEEL OPTIONS

Factory-made wheels are inexpensive, especially the smaller ones. They are usually smooth, strong, and ready to use. If they aren't quite right for your project they can be adapted by adding tread pattern marks, smoothing the tread area, or even coloring them.

If you want a different look (or don't want to go shopping for wheels), you can make the wheels for the car. This allows you to choose the wood type and color, as well as wheel diameter and width. Clearly this will take much more time than attaching factory-made wheels, but you are a woodworker, and the wheels are fun to make.

## FACTORY-MADE WHEELS

Contour wheels are available in diameters of ½ in., ⅝ in., ¾ in., and larger. These three smaller sizes are each available with ⅛ in. holes. They are inexpensive and very easy to use—no modifications needed. They can be stained or colored easily. However, if you need to order them in, you may end up waiting a week or so.

**A variety of toy wheels**

**Factory-made wheels**

Modified contour wheel     Stained contour wheel

Dual contour wheel     Modified treaded wheel

## MODIFIED FACTORY-MADE WHEELS

These wheels are as described earlier, but with a few simple modifications that may make them better suited to a car depending on your preferences. They can be sized, or treads added, quite easily.

### Contour wheels with flat treads, or two contour wheels made into one wide wheel

To do this you will need a #6 machine screw (a threaded bolt, not a wood screw), at least 1½ in. long (and a couple #6 hex nuts) to make a mandrel for the drill press. The diameter of this small bolt is .130 in., which is a hair over the .125 (⅛) in. hole in the factory-made wheel, so size it as follows:

**1** **Cut the head off the machine screw** (not strictly necessary, but makes it a bit quicker to use). Put the machine screw in the drill press chuck, and with the chuck turning at a moderate speed, lightly file the tips off the thread teeth until it fits the ⅛ in. hole in the wheel. This only takes a few light strokes with the file because you are only removing .005 in. (an amount equivalent to the thickness of a piece of paper) from the tips of the threads.

**2** **Check the sizing of the mandrel by** sliding on a wheel.

**3** If wanting wider contour wheels, glue two contour wheels together. Use the mandrel as a clamp, and be generous with the glue so it squeezes out a little all around. Have the flat sides together to form the glued joint.

**4** Put the mandrel in the drill press, and file the outside diameter until it is flat and about $^{11}/_{16}$ in. diameter. You can use a large rasp for this, which will likely leave treadlike grooves. Do the same thing with a single wheel, if that is the width of wheel you need.

**5** You can also use a smaller smooth file, and then file tread grooves with the corner of a file. These grooves tend to hide the glue line, but are optional.

**6** Sand the surface and round the sharp corners. Go through the same filing and sanding process for the front single wheels.

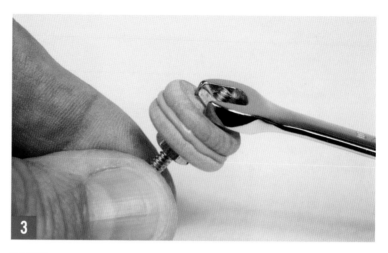

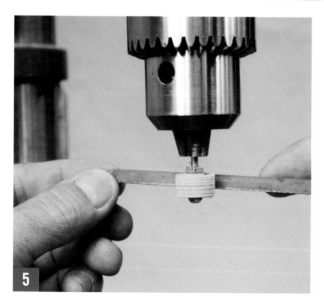

# HOLE SAW WHEELS

These are the most work, but end up with a center hub a different color than the rest of the wheel, which can be an attractive option. However, it takes careful work to drill the axle hole exactly on center. I generally make twice as many wheels as I need, and pick the best four. This is very little extra work to do while the tools are set up. A ¾ in. hole saw makes ⅝ in. diameter wheels. A ⅝ in. hole saw makes ½ in. diameter wheels. A good rule of thumb is ⅜ in. width for the rear wheels, and ¼ in. for the front.

**1** Get a block of a hardwood of your choice. This needs to be at least 1 in. wide, at least ¾ in. thick, and at least 4 in. long. To make extra wheels, you will need two blocks, or a larger block. Drill two holes for the larger wheels on one half of the block and two holes for the smaller wheels on the other half. Each should be between ⅜ in. and ½ in. deep.

**2** Glue ¼ in. dowel in the holes; they should protrude slightly.

**3** Sand or plane the dowels flush with the wheels.

**4** Carefully locate center on each wheel; make a center dimple with an awl.

**5** Drill ⅛ in. holes in the dowels, at least ½ in. deep.

**6** Saw wheels from block. Sand on drill press mandrel (see page 12).

# PLUG CUTTER WHEELS

A nice set of plug cutters allows for cutting fairly long plugs (1½ in.). The plugs need to be at least ¾ in. long to work well. You are essentially making your own short dowels.

The plugs can be drilled into end grain or flat grain. Most factory wheels are end grain, and this is slightly stronger than flat or edge grain; however, either works as long as the wood is a good hardwood with fine grain.

**1** **Select the wood that suits you. Make** plugs as long as possible, so the wood needs to be at least 1 in. thick and large enough for two larger rear wheel plugs and two smaller front wheel plugs. Drill the plugs. Saw to maximum length to create short pieces of dowel.

**2** **Cut plug to length using miter gauge** on bandsaw as shown on page 15. Use the jig (page 15) to drill the plugs on center. This can be done on a drill press or with a portable drill. Saw plugs to make wheels (see photo top of page 15), then sand on drill press mandrel to smooth and round the corners as shown on page 12.

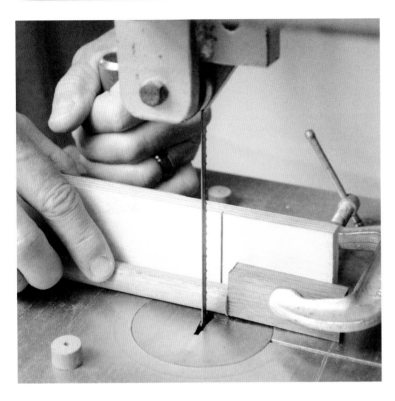

## DOWEL WHEELS

These wheels can be made simply, using the drilling jig as shown on page 15. The big advantage is that dowel stock is readily available. The only disadvantage is the limited choice of dowel wood species, and therefore limited color choice (though you can have your choice if you have access to a plug cutter). Once the dowel is drilled, it can be carefully sawn off using a miter gauge and a bandsaw. Grip the dowel firmly to keep it from spinning as you cut.

## JIG FOR DRILLING AXLE HOLES IN DOWELS OR PLUGS

Each jig will end up about 1 in. square by about 2 inches long. The block of maple in the photo is about 2 x 2 x 8 in. long. Mark out the squares and hole centers. Exact size is not important.

**1** Drill a hole to match the wheel size, about half as deep as the length of the plugs, then switch to a ⅛ in. drill bit without moving the setup, if possible.

**2** Drill the ⅛ in. guide hole, at least ¾ in. deeper than the existing larger hole.

**3** Saw the jig blocks to separate them.

# MONSTER TRUCK TRACTOR TREADS

You can mark out treads and saw them to imitate the tractor tires generally used by monster trucks (see page 76). Two wheels or wheel slabs are glued together to form one wide tractor wheel. One wheel will have treads angled to the right, the other wheel to the left; they will form the V tread when assembled.

**1** Remove the factory treads. A disc sander works surprisingly well. Sand lightly, then check. If not sanded perfectly evenly, you will see some tread remaining; keep sanding to remove those tread marks.

**2** Use the Monster Truck Tractor Tire Fixture on page 18 to make this angled block. It supports the wheel while cutting the treads on the bandsaw. The ¼ in. dowels locate the wheels while allowing them to rotate. One pin allows cutting of the left half of the treads, and the other pin allows cutting of the right half.

**3** Mark out the tread locations, using the template from page 17. Do this on all eight wheels. They will be glued together in pairs. These wheels have 24 treads, but 16 is fine too, and slightly faster to make. Make a pencil dot to mark the cut location.

**4** Set up to cut treads on four of the wheels. Set a stop so the treads will all be the same depth (whatever you choose between $\frac{1}{32}$ and $\frac{1}{16}$ in.). It is useful to have another guide fence clamped in place to keep the fixture located as you move in and out of the very short cut.

**5** Saw the treads on four wheels. Do a trial run to find the best location for the cut. If the wheel is moved slightly off center, the cut may have a more even depth across the face of the wheel. The spacing will not be exact, but it will be close enough to look good when the wheels are assembled.

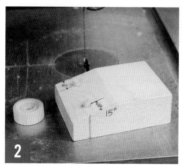

**6** Set up to cut the opposite angle treads on the other four wheels. The depth stop can remain as-is, but the side fence is moved from left to right, and the angled fixture is reversed as well.

**7** Saw the treads on the remaining four wheels.

**8** Sand to remove all sharp edges.

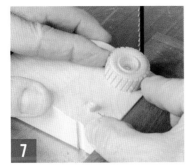
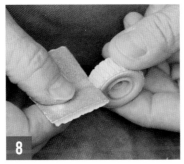

**9** Glue the wheel pairs together. You will want two left-hand wheels and two right-hand wheels. The best clamping method is to use a ¼ in. bolt to align and clamp the wheel halves together. If no bolt is handy, use a length of ¼ in. dowel to align the two wheels. Glue the flat sides together. Hold the wheels together for a minute, then carefully remove the dowel (there might be a little squeeze-out glue that will bond the dowel to the wheels, so remove it while you still can) and clamp the wheels.

24 tractor treads

16 tractor treads

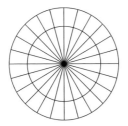
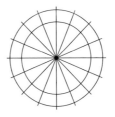

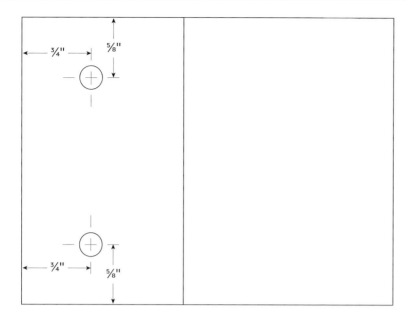

**Monster truck "tractor"
tires fixture**
3" W x 4" L x 1" T

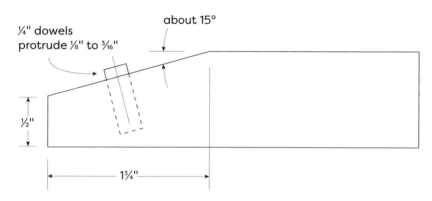

¼" dowels
protrude ⅛" to 3⁄16"

about 15°

½"

1¾"

Notes:
Exact length, width, and
thickness are not critical.
Angle can be anywhere
between a couple degrees
either side of 15.

# OFF-ROAD KNOBBY TIRES

These tires can be paired as "duals" for
the monster truck (page 76). This is a
similar but quicker process versus that
used to make the tractor treads.

**1** **For these wheels, leave the factory
treads in place;** don't sand them off as
is done for the tractor-style wheels. Mark
out the cross-tread spacing (see tractor
tread wheels, page 16, step 3). Set a depth
stop on the bandsaw. The cut will be
between 1⁄32 and 1⁄16 in. deep.

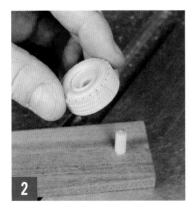

**2** Prepare to saw the treads. You may want to use a very simple fixture (a short dowel glued into a scrap of wood) to help hold the wheels safely.

**3** Keep your fingers to the sides of the blade and use gentle pressure only.

**4** Sand to remove burrs or sharp corners.

**5** If making dual wheels, glue the wheels together in pairs.

# DRILLING DOWEL HOLES

Because dowels vary in size, you can't assume that a ⅛ in. diameter dowel will fit perfectly in a hole drilled with a ⅛ in. drill bit. It is a good idea to drill a test hole in scrap and see if the dowel you are using for a particular project fits; if not, you have two options. You could chuck the dowel into your drill press and use fine sandpaper on the last ¼ in. to make it a bit skinnier, as shown (takes about two seconds); or you could pick the next slightly larger drill bit.

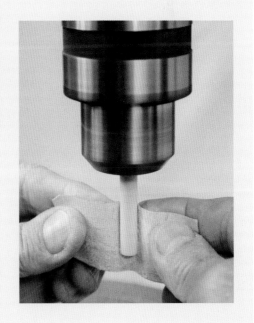

When drilling longer holes that need to be straight, there are a few tips to keep in mind. You can drill right through from one side, or halfway through from each side. The latter reduces the chance of the bit "wandering" as it goes through varying wood grain. Try drilling first on a scrap of similar wood. Clamp the wood to the drill press table securely and set a depth stop, or mark the drill bit with masking tape. Use a high-speed RPM and a low feed rate, and clear the chips often.

# FINISHING

Generally it is best to finish the wheels separately from the rest of the toy. The finish quality is better, and any excess glue can easily be removed when assembling the toy later. Unfinished wheels tend to get glue stains that are hard to remove. However, make sure to plug the axle holes. Finish there will reduce glue strength. See notes on finishing, page 23.

# ASSEMBLY

The assembly procedure is the same for factory-made wheels and custom-made wheels.

**1** **Cut the dowel axles to length, allowing** for at least ⅟₃₂ in. end clearance for the wheels to run freely. Sand the ends smooth or slightly rounded. Test the fit of the dowels and wheels. It is not unusual to have to sand the diameter of the dowel very slightly. Dab finish on the ends of the axles. This prevents stains from glue during assembly.

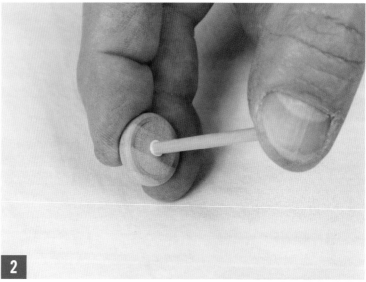

**2** **Place glue in the wheel holes using** a toothpick, and also put a tiny bit of glue on the end of the axle where the wheel will sit. Press into place and wipe off the excess glue. The wheel is finished already, so the glue will wipe off easily. For the larger wheels such as the monster trucks, have a small mallet handy just in case the glue swells the axle slightly and the wheel sticks.

**3** **Rub a little paraffin wax on the center** area of the axle and on the ends of the axle housings. This will reduce friction and help keep any excess glue from adhering and freezing the axles and wheels.

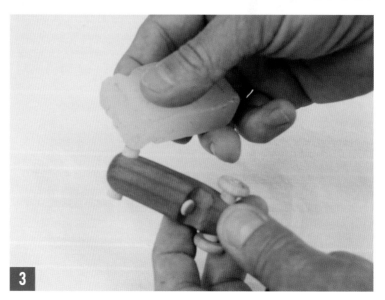

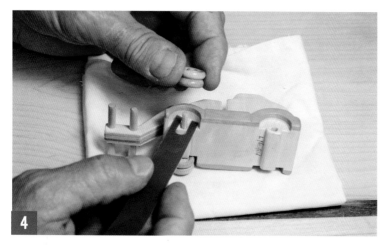

**4** **If the toy has more than two axles,** dry-fit the wheels and axles in place and check that the wheels all turn when the toy is moved along a flat surface. If the surface is slippery, place a piece of paper on the surface then try again. If one axle isn't turning, you may need to drill out the holes in the toy to allow a little more clearance for the axles. Hold a small spacer "tool" (you can make one out of a coffee can's plastic lid) between the wheel and the axle housing to make sure there will be a small gap after assembly.

**5** **When the wheels all contact the play** surface, glue the other wheels into place. Put glue in the wheel and on the axle end after it is in the axle housing. Press or tap the wheel in place. Spin the wheels in a couple of minutes to make sure that any unseen glue squeeze-out doesn't freeze the axle in place.

## PROJECT NOTES

The pickup truck (page 26) has extra-detailed instructions to show the common steps of most toys. Take a look at it for pointers if you decide to build another toy first.

# PLANE STANDS

Toy planes often sit on a shelf or in a box. However, sometimes a child (or adult) may want to display them. While wheeled toys display very nicely on their own, planes look better up off the ground. These stands are very simple: just a base and a mounting dowel.

**1 Mark out the base block. The base is** ⅜ in. or ½ in.-thick solid wood or plywood, about 2½ in. long by 1½ in. wide. For safety in cutting, use a larger piece. This base can be rectangular, oval, round, or any shape you desire. Mark a dowel hole ¾ in. from one end and drill it. The wood is clamped at a slight angle so the dowel is angled, making the toy look more dynamic.

**2 Saw the block to the finished** dimensions, then sand the cut surfaces to remove saw marks.

**3 Cut a length of dowel about 3 in. long.** Sand a bevel on the top end so the plane will easily slip over the dowel. Glue the dowel to the base.

**4 Apply a finish. You may decide to stain** the stand assembly a dark color if you want it to contrast with a lighter-colored plane. Finally, on the plane, drill a small hole under the wing toward the front of the fuselage and square to the fuselage. This lets the plane naturally rest with the nose pointed slightly up when it is placed on the stand's angled dowel.

# FINISHING

Wood toys should have a durable, safe finish. It needs to be reasonably easy to apply, and I have found that glossy toys are best received. Here are four general guidelines when choosing a finish:

1. **The finish must be safe.** While the children who will play with these toys are probably old enough that chewing on the toys is unlikely, it is still a possibility in any household with young children around. Fortunately, many finishes answer this requirement, from salad bowl finishes to hard finishes that are safe after curing.

2. **The finish should be durable.** A finish that wears off quickly will not protect the toy from moisture or general wear and tear.

3. **The finish should be easy to apply.** Small toys present some problems in finishing, notably small corners and recesses.

4. **The finish should look great.** I have found out that for kids, this means smooth and glossy. Perhaps gloss appeals because most (though not all) cars, trucks, planes, and boats have shiny finishes. I have made toys using satin, semi-gloss, and gloss finishes; gloss is the consistent favorite.

## SPRAY FINISH TIPS

After trying a variety of spray-, brush-, and rag-applied finishes, I recommend using spray finish with UV protection and a high-gloss finish. Most topcoats are non-toxic when cured, but some such finishes develop runs and sags much more easily than others. Because finishes come and go, I suggest trying several kinds and using the most run-resistant.

Spray the moving parts, such as wheels or propellers, separately from the toy body. This allows easy access to the wheel wells or airplane nose sections for finishing, as well as both sides of the

wheel or propeller. This also keeps the axles from sticking later.

It is useful to make a spraying stand to hold the toy and prevent it from sticking to surfaces while it dries. A few nails driven into a scrap piece of 2 x 4 will do the trick (top photo).

Set the wheels on short pieces of axle dowel and stand the dowel upright on an upside-down cardboard box (bottom photo). The dowel plugs the axle hole to keep finish out (if it is a snug fit) and serves to keep the wheels up off the surface.

## STAINS & COLORING

I rarely use stain, paint, or dye. I prefer to use wood that is an appropriate color where possible and leave the wood its natural color. I have tried staining wood wheels black, but prefer the natural maple color. However, I did use yellow food coloring to make a school bus into a traditional yellow color and it turned out well (see top left of page 7).

# LAND

This first section is jam-packed with toys of the wheeled variety. From car-crunching monster trucks to speedy dragsters to hardworking haulers, you'll find 12 vehicles to park in your toy garage.

# PICKUP TRUCK

This simple pickup truck is a great place to start your toy-making journey. The instructions are extra-detailed here to help walk you through the common steps you'll see in most projects. When you're done, you'll have a rough-and-tumble pickup perfect for toting just about anything you can think of. The trailer hitch hole allows for even more hauling capacity by adding the flat deck or RV trailers (page 32; 39).

## CUT LIST

| NO. REQ'D | PART NAME | MATERIAL | T" | W" | L" | NOTES |
|---|---|---|---|---|---|---|
| 1 | Body | Hardwood | 1¼ | 1¼ | 3 | |
| 4 | Wheels | ⅝ in. factory-made contour | | | | For custom wheels, see pages 10 to 21 for instructions. |
| 2 | Axles | ⅛ in. dowel | | | To suit. | |

## ASSEMBLY GUIDE & TEMPLATES

**Side**
(bolded line)

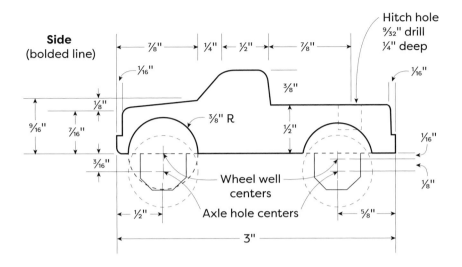

Hitch hole
⁹⁄₃₂" drill
¼" deep

⅞"  ¼"  ½"  ⅞"

¹⁄₁₆"

⅛"

⁹⁄₁₆"  ⁷⁄₁₆"

³⁄₁₆"

½"

⅜" R

³⁄₈"

½"

¹⁄₁₆"

⅛"

⁵⁄₈"

Wheel well centers

Axle hole centers

3"

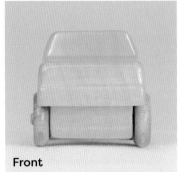

**Front**

**Back**

**Back**

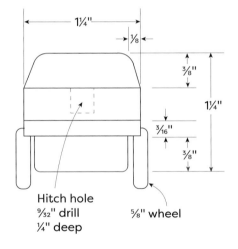

1¼"

⅛"

³⁄₈"

1¼"

³⁄₁₆"

³⁄₈"

Hitch hole
⁹⁄₃₂" drill
¼" deep

⅝" wheel

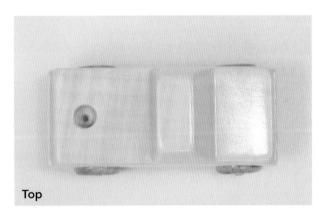

**Top**

**Side**

# TRUCK BODY

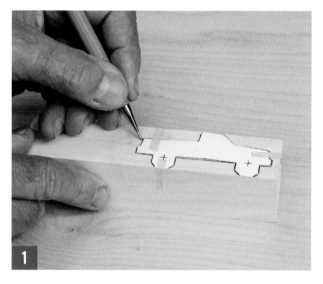

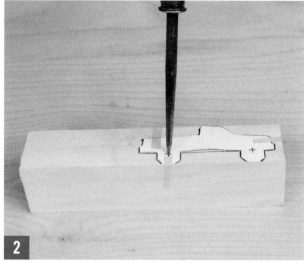

**1** **Select the wood. It needs to be** 1¼ x 1¼ x 3 in. long. Best to have it an inch or two longer if possible to allow for easier and safer cutting. Mark out the side profile, using the template (see page 27).

**2** **Mark the wheel well centers using** an awl.

**3** **Mark out the wheel well centers on the** other side, accurately as possible. Use a square to continue the wheel well center locations around the bottom and up the other side, then measure the distance up from the bottom. If the wheel well holes are significantly different side to side, the wheels may rub or look quite off-center.

**4** **Saw the truck bottom contour. Do this** now, while the profile lines are still visible (they are partially removed when drilling the wheel wells).

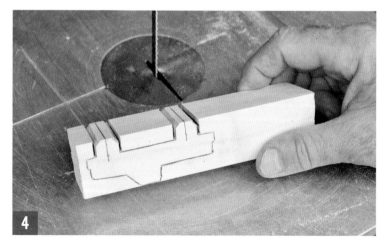

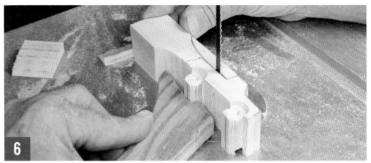

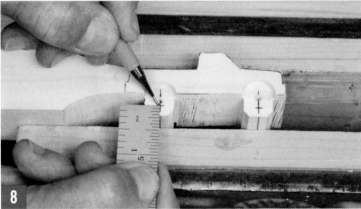

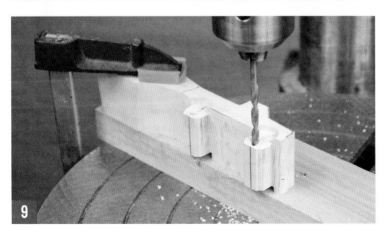

**5** Drill the four wheel wells. Use a ⅝ in.-diameter flat bottom drill to make a ⅛ in.-deep recess. Shown is a Forstner-style bit, but a brad-point bit would work well also.

**6** Saw most of the side profile. Leave a "handle" section if possible.

**7** Smooth the axle ends. Use a small sharp chisel or saw to trim the excess corners of the wheel wells, then file or sand the end surfaces flat.

**8** Mark out the axle hole centers. Both should be ³⁄₁₆ in. up from the bottom, and in line vertically with the wheel well centers. Or, measuring down from the existing wheel well centers, the front axle center will be ³⁄₁₆ in. below and the rear axle ⅛ in. below the wheel well center.

**9** Drill the axle holes. This step depends on the wheels you use. The wheels pictured have a ⅛ in. hole, so required ⅛ in. dowel axles. This means drilling the holes ⁵⁄₃₂ in. Use a high rpm and a slow feed to help keep the drill from wandering. Clear the chips a few times, as needed.

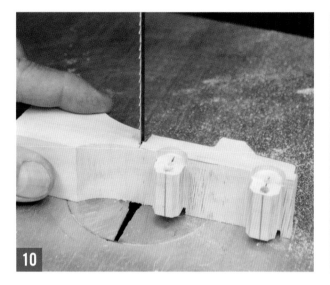

**10** Finish sawing the truck. Remove the truck from the excess wood.

**11** Mark out the side window angle. Measure or estimate a line ⅛ in. from the side edges on the roof, and angle down to the bottom of the windshield.

**12** Saw the angles.

**13** Remove all saw marks. File and sand each surface until smooth.

**14** Remove all sharp corners and edges. Round over the hood and roof areas, ending up with a radius of about ¹⁄₁₆ in. on those surfaces and slightly less on the truck box edges.

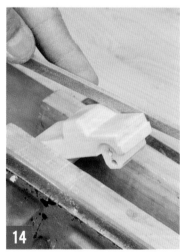

**15** Mark out the location of the trailer hitch hole. It is ⅝ in. from the back of the truck, and on center sideways.

**16** Drill the 9⁄32 in. hole that is ¼ in. deep. This diameter allows 1⁄32 in. clearance on the ¼ in. trailer hitch dowel.

**17** Finish-sand all surfaces.

## COMPLETING

The truck in the photos has factory ⅝ in.-diameter wheels with ⅛ in. holes. See pages 10 to 21 for information on other wheel options. See page 23 for finishing information.

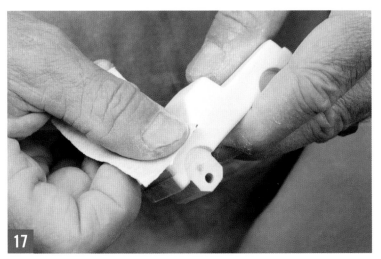

# FIFTH-WHEEL FLAT DECK TRAILER

Simply drop the dowel hitch of this fifth-wheel flat deck trailer in place behind your pickup truck to triple its hauling capacity (page 26). The handy lip around the edge of the trailer helps your cargo stay in place around sharp corners and over treacherous routes.

## CUT LIST

| NO. REQ'D | PART NAME | MATERIAL | T" | W" | L" | NOTES |
|---|---|---|---|---|---|---|
| 2 | Frame sides | Baltic birch plywood | ⅛ | 1⅛ | 6⅛ | |
| 1 | Frame center: Front | Hardwood | ¼ | ⅜ | 1⅛ | Cut at least 4½ in. long to make rear piece also. |
| 1 | Frame center: Rear | Hardwood | ¼ | ⅜ | 3½ | See note above. |
| 1 | Deck | Baltic birch plywood | ⅛ | 1¾ | 4½ | Rough-cut ⅛ in. over length and width. |
| 1 | Deck rim | Baltic birch plywood | ⅛ | 1¾ | 4½ | Rough-cut ⅛ in. over length and width. |
| 1 | Axle block | Hardwood | ⅜ | 1 | 1¼ | |
| 1 | Hitch pin | ¼ in. dowel | | | To suit. | Rough-cut about ¾ in. long. |
| 4 | Wheels | ⅝ in. factory-made contour | | | | See pages 10 to 21 for custom wheel information. |
| 2 | Axles | ⅛ in. dowel | | | To suit. | |

*Note: Dimensions are finished sizes. Most parts should be rough-cut oversize. See instructions.*

## ASSEMBLY GUIDE

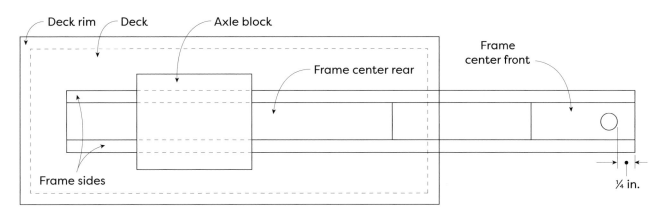

- Deck rim
- Deck
- Axle block
- Frame center rear
- Frame center front
- Frame sides
- ¼ in.

## TEMPLATES

**Side**

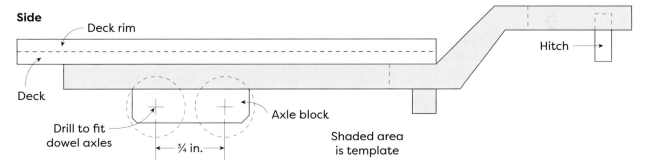

- Deck rim
- Deck
- Hitch
- Drill to fit dowel axles
- ¾ in.
- Axle block
- Shaded area is template

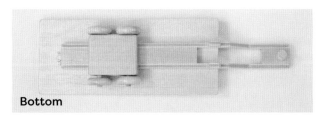

**Bottom**

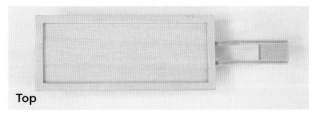

**Top**

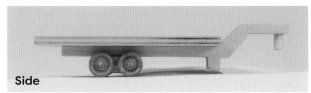

**Side**

**Front**

**Back**

# FRAME SIDES

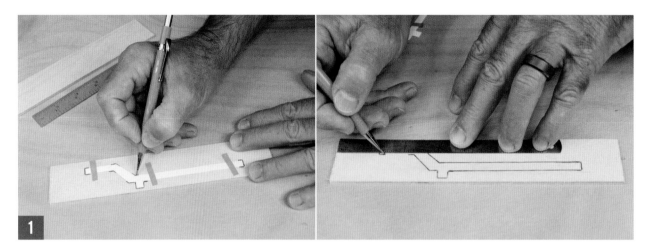

**1** Cut two pieces of ⅛ in.-thick plywood. These should be at least 7 in. long by at least 1⅛ in. wide. Mark out the profile on one piece. Mark out the corner locations, then use a straightedge to join.

**2** Temporarily glue the two pieces together. This will allow you to saw matching pieces. Put dabs of glue on the reverse side, in the corners, and in places that will be removed when sawing the profile. Clamp together.

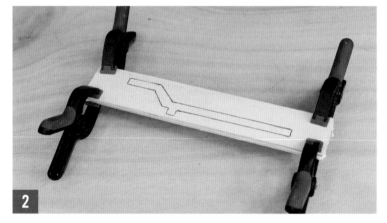

**3** Apply masking tape to the bottom. This reduces chipping from the saw. Saw the frame profile. Leave ⅟₃₂ to ⅟₁₆ in. extra wood on both sides of the horizontal cuts, but saw the angled "gooseneck" surfaces as accurately and closely to the line as possible. Plan your cuts so the pieces stay glued together until the last cut.

## FRAME CENTER PIECES

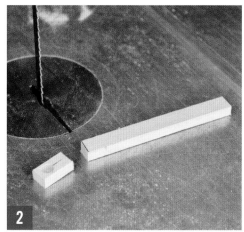

**1** **Cut the strip of ¼ in.-thick wood. You** need at least 4½ in.: one piece is ¾ in. long, the other 3½ in. Mark out the hitch hole ¼ in. from one end. Select the drill bit to fit your ¼ in. dowel (see page 19). Drill ³⁄₁₆ in. deep. You can drill right through if you don't mind the hitch dowel showing on top.

**2** **Saw the two pieces to length.**

**3** **Sand the ends smooth and flat. Use** a disc sander or a piece of sandpaper on a flat surface.

## FRAME ASSEMBLY

**1** **Glue the two center pieces to one** side of the frame. Center them on the plywood frame.

**2** **Attach the second side, aligning it as** closely as possible with the first. Check by eye that it protrudes the same amount on each side as the first does. Sand or file the top and bottom surfaces flush. Use a coarse grit, then a fine grit. Lastly, use a small smooth file for details. The deck attaches to the top, and the axle block to the bottom of the longer section. Keep these surfaces flat and straight.

# DECK

**1** Cut the ⅛ in. plywood. You need two pieces that are 2 x 4¾ in. This is ⅛ in. oversize for now. One piece provides the platform; the other forms a thin rim to keep cargo from falling off. On one piece, draw a line ¼ in. in from the edge all around. This will produce an opening that is 4¼ x 1½ in.

**2** Saw to the line. As with the frame, put masking tape on the back surface to reduce chipping. After drilling an access hole, use a scroll saw or coping saw to carefully cut close to the line.

**3** Sand or file the inside cuts. Keep the tape on, remove saw marks, and straighten the cuts if needed. If you use a smooth small file in the corners, be careful not to chip out the back edge, or file a small bevel on the back edge first. Sand the deck surface if needed, then glue on the border, keeping outside edges flush. Remove squeeze-out with a small sharp chisel as soon as the glue is rubbery.

**4** When the glue is dry, mark out a line ³⁄₁₆ in. out from the inside of the border. Sand to the line. If needed, you may want to first saw off some excess. Hand-sand to smooth and remove all sharp corners. Glue the deck to the frame. Check that it is centered on the frame, front and back.

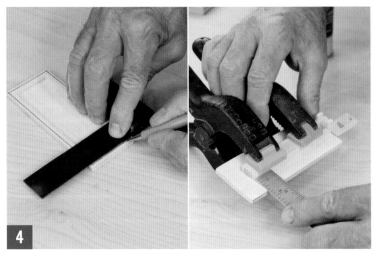

# AXLE BLOCK

The sizes here are assuming the trailer is to be fitted to the pickup truck, and that the pickup truck box top is the same height as the design in this book. If you have put a "lift kit" on the truck, or used different-sized wheels, then you may need to allow for this by increasing the thickness of the axle housing.

**1** Cut the ⅜ in.-thick block to size. Final size is 1 in. wide x 1¼ long. Sand the ends flat and square to the sides. Bevel the sharp corners, except where they will contact the frame.

**2** Glue the axle block to the underside of the trailer. Have it centered side to side and square to the deck edge.

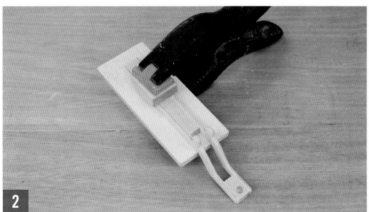

**3** Place the truck and trailer on a flat surface. Shim the trailer up so it is level and the hitch is about ⅛ in. above the truck box. The trailer is shown clamped to a straight off-cut with a shim of ⅛ in.-thick plywood under the trailer. For ⅝ in.-diameter wheels, the center is ⁵⁄₁₆ in. up from the "ground," so the line will need to be ³⁄₁₆ in. up from the bottom of the axle block (⁵⁄₁₆ in. minus the ⅛ in. shim). The axle centers are ¾ in. apart. Mark with an awl.

**4** Drill the holes. Clamp the deck to a squared-up block of wood as shown, or swivel the drill press table to 90°. The photo shows a spacer block under the trailer to keep it level. Sometimes a small drill tends to wander, so use a sharp bit, high RPM, and a slow feed, clearing the chips often.

## HITCH PIN

**1** **The hitch pin length determines the** height of the trailer gooseneck. It will bottom out in the pickup's hitch hole, so the first thing you need to do is calculate the length needed. Add ⅛ in. for the desired gap, then add the depth of the hole in the trailer (close to ³⁄₁₆ in.). Add ¹⁄₃₂ to ¹⁄₁₆ in. for a safety margin. The dowel can be shortened after assembly if needed.

**2** **Cut the dowel to length. Sand the cut** end to remove sharp corners.

**3** **Glue the hitch dowel into the trailer** gooseneck hole, applying the glue into the hole with a toothpick.

## COMPLETING

Shown are factory-made ⅝ in.-diameter wheels with ⅛ in. holes. You could make your own wheels if desired. See pages 10 to 21 for information on making and assembling wheels. See page 23 for information on finishing.

# FIFTH-WHEEL RV TRAILER

This trailer is a natural fit with the pickup truck (page 26). This toy has an optional interior, which makes the trailer look a little better, and makes it slightly lighter in weight. However, you may skip the interior details if you like. Either way, hitch up and get ready to travel the country!

## CUT LIST

| NO. REQ'D | PART NAME | MATERIAL | T" | W" | L" | NOTES |
|---|---|---|---|---|---|---|
| 1 | Trailer body center | Hardwood or softwood | 1 | 2 ½ | 6 ¼ | |
| 2 | Trailer body sides | Hardwood or softwood | ¼ | 2 ½ | 6 ¼ | Note grain direction. See instructions. |
| 1 | Hitch pin | ¼ in. dia. dowel | | | To fit. | At least ⅝ in. long. |
| 2 | Jack pins | ¼ in. dia. dowel | | | To fit. | At least ½ in. long. |
| 2 | Axles | ⅛ in. dia. dowel | | | To fit. | At least 2 ⅝ in. long. |
| 4 | Wheels | ⅝ in. dia. factory-made contour | | | | ⅛ in. axle holes |

*Note: Dimensions are finished sizes. Most parts should be rough-cut oversize. See instructions.*

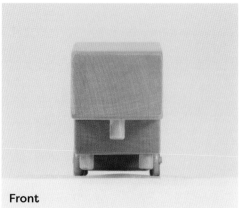

Front

Back

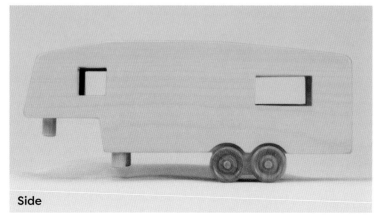

Side

## TEMPLATES

**Right side**

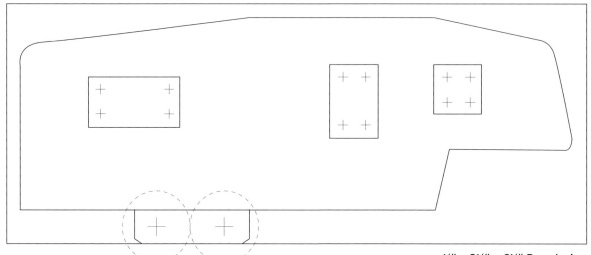

¼" x 2½" x 6¼" Rough size

## Interior

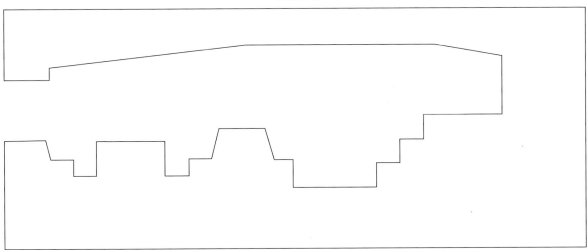

1" x 2½" x 6¼" Rough size

## Left side

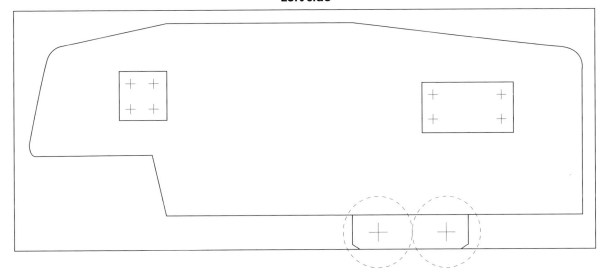

## Bottom
Dowel hole locations

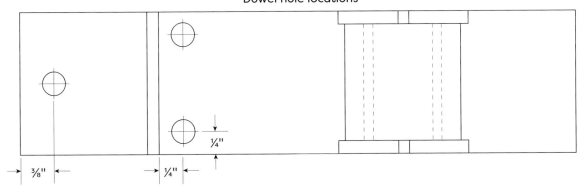

# BODY CENTER

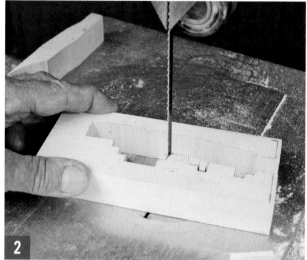

**1** Select the wood. The rough size of the block should be 1 in. thick and at least 2½ in. wide by at least 6¼ long. If using ⅛ in.-thick sides, the interior block should be 1¼ in. thick.

**2** Mark out the interior contour. Trace the template, or measure it out. If not sawing out interior details, skip to the Sides section. Saw the interior contours.

**3** Smooth the saw cuts. Use a small fine-tooth file, then do minimal sanding to remove sharp corners. Round any corners slightly.

**4** Spray-finish the interior. Mask off the sides, then apply the finish.

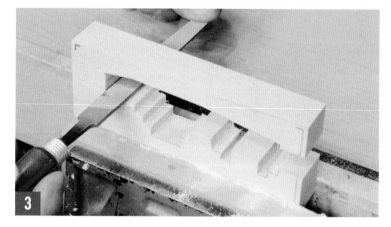

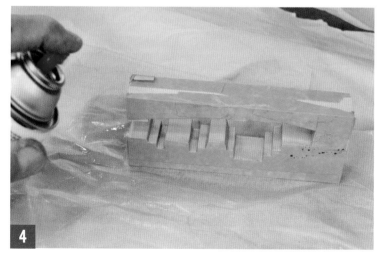

# SIDES

**PROJECT NOTES**

The sides are ¼ in. thick and at least 2½ in. wide by at least 6¼ long. The right-hand side has an extra window, representing the door window. Of course, the windows can be sized and located however you like.

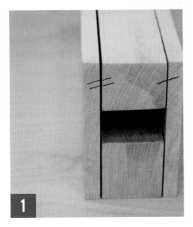

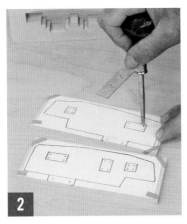

**1** Mark the location of the sides and center block. This will help keep the parts oriented throughout the different processes. Prepare the template. You can pencil in the back side to turn it into makeshift carbon paper. Trace the window outlines, and mark the window hole centers with an awl. Use a red ballpoint pen with a ruler to mark the contour. The red color makes it easy to see which lines you have traced.

**2** Mark the axle and window hole centers. Each window has a hole in the corner to make sawing easier, and each axle will be drilled later also. If you don't have a ¾ in. flat-bottom drill, then use a compass to draw the ⅜ in.-radius wheel wells. They can be sawn out instead.

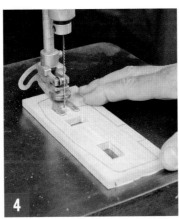

**3** Masking tape reduces the amount of chip-out on the underside when sawing. Drill the window corner holes. The centers are located ⅛ in. from the window edges, but instead of using a ¼ in. drill bit, try a 3/16 or 7/32 in., which allows a tiny bit of clearance from the window edge.

**4** Saw the window openings. Saw very carefully along the lines. Accurate cutting here will reduce the amount of filing and sanding needed. File or sand a small bevel on the corners to reduce splintering, then use a small file to remove the sawing marks.

**5** Remove the sharp edges around the windows. Sand both sides of the window openings.

## ASSEMBLY

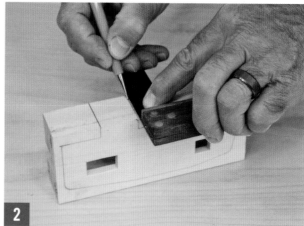

1 **If you omit the interior cutouts, darken** the areas behind the window openings to give the idea of depth. Mask off the sides so only the window areas are stained. Stain and let dry. Glue one side in place. Apply glue all around the perimeter, but be sparing near the window openings to avoid squeeze-out.

2 **Draw location lines for the second side.** Carry the axle housing lines across the bottom of the trailer, and do the same on the remaining ¼ in.-thick side so you can align the sides exactly.

3 **Glue the second side in place. Line up** the two sides as carefully as possible. Have the axles directly across from each other.

4 **When the glue is dry, sand the bottom** flat and square to the sides. This allows you to use a square for accurate wheel center layout. Shown is a sanding board with coarse-grit sandpaper.

5 **Mark out the axle centers on the** second side. It is important for this to be accurate or the wheels will look off-center. Carry the centerline across the bottom and up the unmarked side. Measure up from the bottom to match the first side layout.

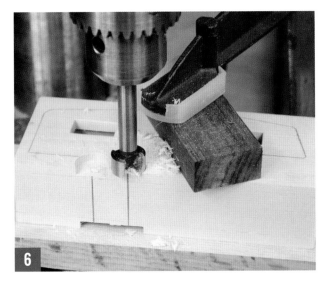

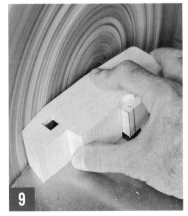

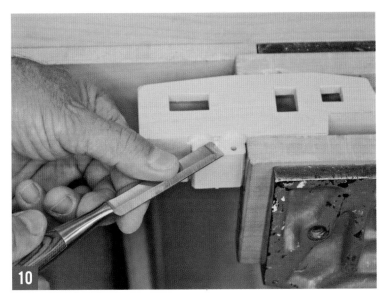

**6** Drill out the wheel wells. The depth is ⅛ to 5⁄32 in. (about the thickness of the wheel). Use a ¾ in. Forstner bit.

**7** Drill the axle holes. These should be about 1⁄32 in. larger than the axle size. The ⅝ in.-diameter contour wheels shown have ⅛ in. holes, so 5⁄32 in. holes are needed. Use a sharp drill bit, a high RPM, and a low feed rate to keep the drill bit from wandering. Clear the chips often.

**8** Mark out the axle housing lines again. They were removed during drilling.

**9** Saw the outside contour now, before the wheel well drilling removes the axle housing outline. File and sand the outside contour. Start with a machine sander where possible, then remove the saw marks from remaining areas using a small smooth file or sandpaper.

**10** Remove the wheel well's sharp corner with a sharp chisel.

# HITCH PIN & JACK PINS

**PROJECT NOTES**

The jack pins allow the trailer to sit a little more upright when unhitched from the truck. The hitch pin connects the trailer to the truck, but also spaces the trailer up off the truck box. It bottoms out in the pickup box hitch hole to hold up the trailer.

**1** Mark out the hole locations. The jacks are located in the corners, ¼ in. in from both edges. The hitch is ⅜ in. back from the front, and on center side to side. Drill the three holes ¼ in. deep. The trailer is shown clamped to a squared-up wood block, which is then clamped to the drill press table. The scrap of brown wood is a spacer.

**2** The jack pins should protrude about ¼ in. after installation. If the holes are ¼ in. deep, you need pins at least ½ in. long. Longer is fine; they can be trimmed after they are glued. The hitch pin should bottom out in the holes in the truck and trailer, with at least ⅛ in. extra to provide a gap. This pin should likely be cut about ¼ in. overlong for now. Put a little glue in the holes, then press or tap the dowels into place.

**3** Measure the hitch pin's final length. Temporarily install the wheels. Cut a couple ⅛ in. dowel axles about ½ in. or so too long. Likely the trailer will sit up too high at the front. Select a shim (or shims) that bring the trailer up to a level position. Measure the shim thickness.

**4** Saw the measured amount from the hitch pin. Sand to remove the sharp edges on the pin. Sand the trailer, removing all sharp corners and edges.

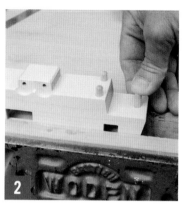

## COMPLETING

This trailer has ⅝ in.-diameter factory-made contour wheels with ⅛ in. holes and axles. See pages 10 to 21 for wheel information. See page 23 for finishing information.

# CAB-OVER TRUCK

The king of the highway, this cab-over truck is ready to move freight through tunnels, over mountains, and cross-country. With details like a grille and exhaust pipe, you'll be ready to hit the road. Make a few to create your own convoy—and don't forget to honk your horn!

## CUT LIST

| NO. REQ'D | PART NAME | MATERIAL | T" | W" | L" | NOTES |
|---|---|---|---|---|---|---|
| 1 | Frame and body block | Hardwood | 1 ¾ | 1 ¾ | 4 ¼ | |
| 1 | Front axle housings | Hardwood | ³⁄₁₆ | ⅜ | 1 ⁹⁄₁₆ | Could be ¼ in. thick. Need at least 7 in. if making trailer (page 54) as well. |
| 2 | Rear axle housings | Hardwood | ³⁄₁₆ | ⅜ | 1 ¹⁄₁₆ | See above note. |
| 1 | Grille (optional) | Veneer | ¹⁄₃₂ | ⅝ | ¾ | |
| 1 | Exhaust | ³⁄₁₆ in. dia. dowel | | | 1 ¾ | |
| 2 | Fuel tanks | ⅜ in. dia. dowel | | | 1 | Rough-cut overlong. See instructions. |
| 10 | Wheels | ¾ in. dia. factory-made contour | | | | Glue rear wheels in pairs to make "duals." See instructions. |
| 3 | Axles | ⅛ in. dowel | | | About 1 ⅞. | Cut length to fit. |

*Note: Dimensions are finished sizes. Most parts should be rough-cut oversize. See instructions.*

Side

Front

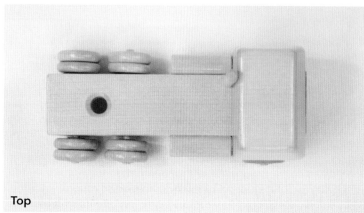

Top

Back

## ASSEMBLY GUIDE

Top

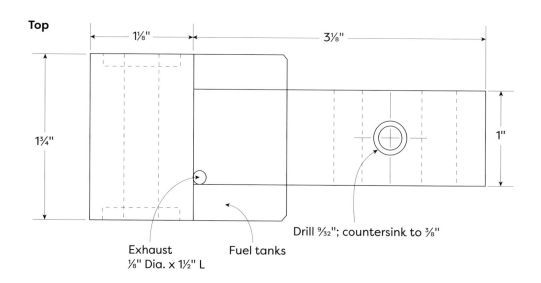

1⅛"

3⅛"

1¾"

1"

Exhaust
⅛" Dia. x 1½" L

Fuel tanks

Drill ⁹⁄₃₂"; countersink to ⅜"

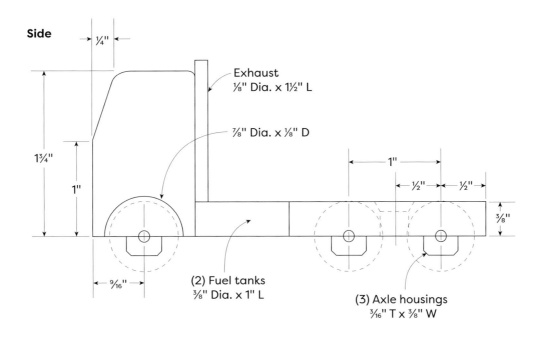

**Side**

¼"

Exhaust
⅛" Dia. x 1½" L

⅞" Dia. x ⅛" D

1"

½"  ½"

1¾"

1"

⅜"

9/16"

(2) Fuel tanks
⅜" Dia. x 1" L

(3) Axle housings
3/16" T x ⅜" W

## SHAPE THE FRAME & BODY BLOCK

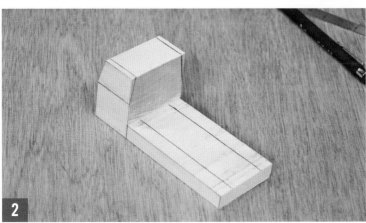

**1** **Cut a block of wood to rough** dimensions (at least 4¼ in. long by 1¾ in. wide by at least 1¾ in. thick). Measure and lay out the side profile. Saw the side contour, including the windshield angle.

**2** **Smooth the saw cuts. If you are using** a disc sander to smooth the cuts, sand the truck front now while the block is mostly intact. It is easier to keep square at this point. Mark out the top profiles. This will include the slight angles for the side windows (⅛ in. in at the top, ¾ in. down on the sides), as well as the 1 in.- wide rear frame. Sand the side window angles. Exact angle is not critical, but keep the cab symmetrical.

**3** Cut the frame to width.

**4** File and sand. Remove the bandsaw marks from the frame cuts. Smooth the back of the cab, keeping it as straight as possible. This will make it simpler to attach the exhaust stack later. Round over the cab roof corners.

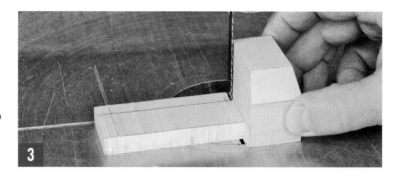

# AXLE HOUSINGS

**1** Cut a length of axle housing wood to ⅜ in. (or up to a maximum of ½ in.) wide by ³⁄₁₆ in. (or up to a maximum of ¼ in.) thick by at least 7 in. long. This will provide enough for the trailer as well as the truck. Bevel the corners slightly by sanding or planing.

**2** Mark the housing length to match the truck width. Axle housings protrude from the truck about ¹⁄₆₄ to ¹⁄₃₂ in. on each end. They can be sanded or filed flush later. Save the leftover for the two axle housings for the trailer (page 54). They should be the same length as the truck axle housings. Use pencil to lightly mark the locations. The front housing should be centered on the cab section, front to back and side to side. The rear axles are spaced with ½ in. between them, and ¼ in. space from the end.

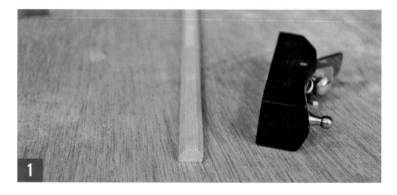

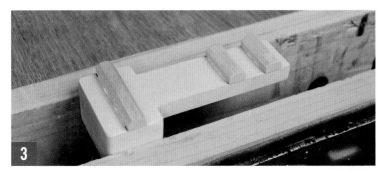

**3** Glue axle housings into place. Have them centered with a slight overhang on each end. Check for location and square. You don't need to clamp these; just press them into place.

**4** When the glue is dry, file or sand the ends flush with the truck.

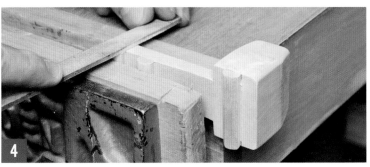

## DRILL THE HOLES

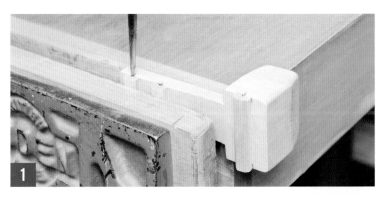

**1** Mark out the hole locations. The front locations will be the centers of the wheel wells. Use an awl to dimple the center locations on both ends of the front housing. The center of the holes will be exactly on the glue joint.

**2** Drill the wheel wells. Grip the truck frame in a drill press vise, or clamp it securely to a square block with a strip of wood to act as a parallel spacer. Drill wheel wells on each side of the cab. Use a Forstner-style drill bit for a flat bottom. This drill bit should be ⅛ in. larger than the wheels. Shown are ¾ in. wheels, so a ⅞ in. drill bit is appropriate. Drill depth should match the thickness of the wheels.

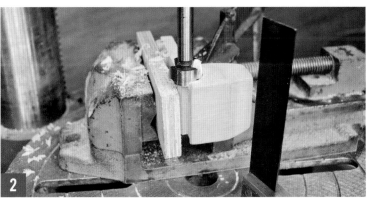

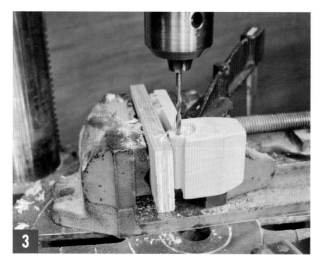

**3** **Drill the front and rear axle holes.** They should be ⁵⁄₃₂ in. This allows ¹⁄₃₂ in. clearance on the ⅛ in. axle dowels.

**4** **Mark out and drill the hitch hole. Drill it** ⁹⁄₃₂ in. This is ¹⁄₃₂ in. larger than the hitch dowel which is ¼ in. diameter.

**5** **Countersink the hole slightly (¹⁄₁₆ in.)** to break the sharp corner and make hitching the trailer easier later. Finish-sand all surfaces. Keep the front as flat as possible for the grille veneer.

# GRILLE (OPTIONAL)

**1** **If the front of the truck looks plain to** you, add the grille. Cut a small rectangle of veneer that contrasts with the truck, approximately ¾ in. long by ⅝ in. wide. It is important to the final appearance that the corners are 90°, but the exact dimensions are not critical. Use scissors; dampen the wood slightly if it tends to crack. Check that the edges are straight and square.

**2** **Spread a thin layer of glue evenly out** to the edges and press the veneer into place. Check that it is set square to the truck front and centered. Clamp gently and evenly. Finish-sand the surface of the grille after the glue has hardened.

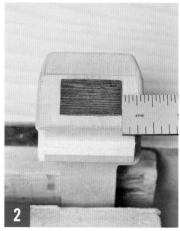

# EXHAUST

**1** **Cut a length of ³⁄₁₆ in.-diameter dowel** 1¾ in. long. It will protrude above the truck ⅛ in. To provide a glue surface, sand or file a small flat about ⅛ in. wide along the length of the dowel.

**2** **Glue in place. Check the fit against the** back of the cab. When satisfied, put a small amount of glue along the dowel flat and press it into place on the cab. Exact location is not critical, but generally at the bottom it sits into the corner between cab and frame, then straight up. Check this best you can with ruler and square—and by eye. Don't try to clamp this; just hold it in place for a minute, then set aside to dry.

# FUEL TANKS

**1** **Plane or sand a flat on a ⅜ in. dowel** at least 2⅛ in. long.

**2** **Cut the dowel to 1 in. lengths, and sand** the ends. Glue to the truck frame. Press in place, then clamp.

## COMPLETING

See page 23 for information on finishing and page 20 for wheel and axle assembly.

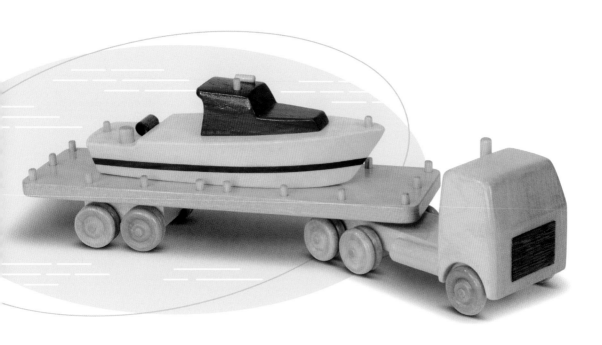

# FLAT DECK TRAILER FOR CAB-OVER TRUCK

10-4! This cab-over trailer has a flat deck that can be made a little longer or shorter. It is designed to carry the Coast Guard boat (page 102), but can haul just about anything that fits! Size it to suit. It is a good idea to have some sort of lip surrounding the deck so the cargo doesn't slide off. This can be short dowel posts as seen here, or a thin rim as used for the fifth-wheel trailer (page 32).

## CUT LIST

| NO. REQ'D | PART NAME | MATERIAL | T" | W" | L" | NOTES |
|---|---|---|---|---|---|---|
| 1 | Deck | Hardwood or Baltic birch plywood | ¼ | 2 | 7 | |
| 18 | Dowel posts | ⅛ in. dowel | | | ⅝ | |
| 1 | Axle block | Hardwood | ½ | 1 | 1½ | |
| 2 | Axle housings | Hardwood | ³⁄₁₆ | ⅜ | 1 ¹⁄₁₆ | Could be ¼ in. thick; see cab-over cutting list page 47. Need at least 2 ½ in. long for trailer only. |
| 1 | Hitch spacer | Hardwood | ⅛ | ¾ | ¾ | |
| 1 | Hitch | ¼ in. dowel | | | ¾ | |
| 8 | Wheels | ¾ in. dia. factory-made contour | | | | Glue rear wheels in pairs to make "duals." See instructions. |
| 2 | Axles | ⅛ in. dowel | | | About 1⅞. | Cut length to fit. |

*Note: Dimensions are finished sizes. Most parts should be rough-cut oversize. See instructions.*

## ASSEMBLY GUIDE

Hitch pin
¼" Dia. x ¾"
L dowel

⅝"

Spacer
⅛" x ¾" x ¾"

**Side**

**Top**

(2) Axle housing
³⁄₁₆" x ⅜" x 1" Lg

1"

Axle holes
⁵⁄₃₂"

Axle block
½" T x 1" W x 1½" Lg

³⁄₁₆"

1"

1"

1"

½"

1"

1"

1¹⁄₁₆"

1¹⁄₁₆"

All holes ⅛" Dia.,
³⁄₁₆" from edge

¼" T x 2" W x 7" L

1"

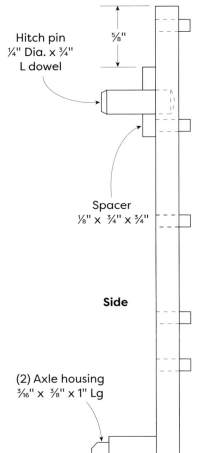

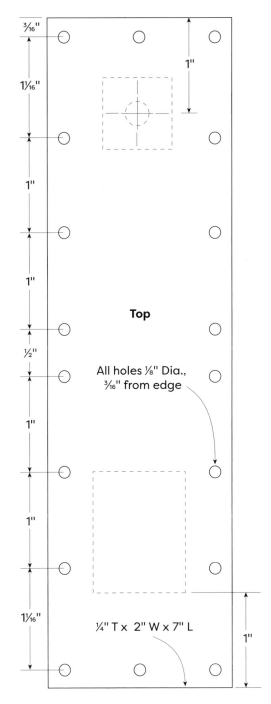

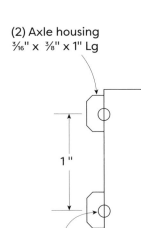
Front

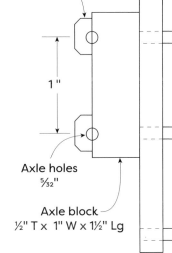
Back

Side

# DECK

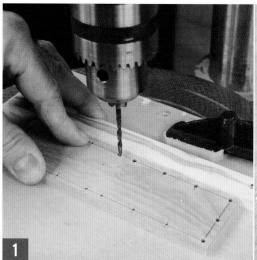

**1** Cut the ¼ in.-thick deck to size (2 in. wide by 7 in. long). Mark out the dowel post locations. Posts located in this particular pattern allow you to haul two monster trucks perfectly. Select a drill bit (see page 19). The dowels will protrude from the bottom about ¹⁄₁₆ in.; you will sand them flush. Create a simple fence to drill the holes. Since all the holes are ³⁄₁₆ in. from the edge, this allows you to push the deck against the fence when drilling.

**2** Cut the dowels to approximately ⅝ in. You will trim them after assembly. Sand and bevel the ends slightly to ease installation. Sand the top surface of the deck; this is much easier now than after the dowels are in. Use a toothpick to put glue in the holes. Push or tap the dowels into place. A piece of ¼ in.-thick wood in the cargo area serves as a spacer to help get all the dowels to the same height.

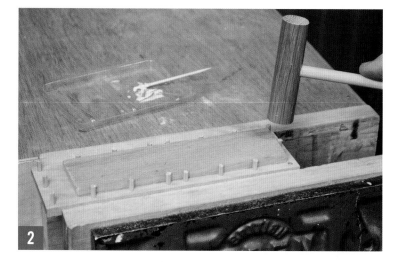

**3** Sand the dowels to final length. Use a sanding board and keep the piece of ⅛ or ³⁄₁₆ in.-thick wood in the cargo area as a spacer to help get all the dowels to the same length. Keep the spacer if you need to hold the deck in a vise for sanding or drilling. Sand the dowel ends slightly to remove sharp edges and provide a slight bevel or round at the tops of the dowels.

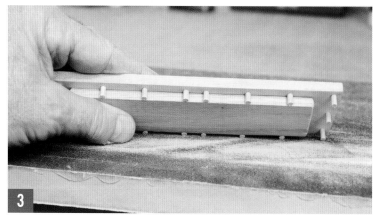

# AXLE BLOCK

**1** **Cut the block to size. It will be 1½ in.** long by 1 in. wide by ½ in. thick. The block is the same color as the wheels. Sand the sides and ends. Glue the block into location. Check that it is centered and square to the deck. Exact placement front to back is not as important.

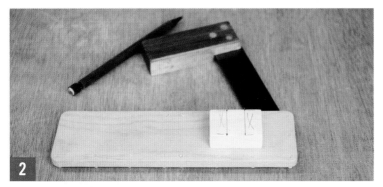

**2** **Mark out axle housing locations. It is** awkward to check for square when the housings are in place, so make small pencil lines now. Glue axle housings in place. Be generous with the glue and firmly press them into location.

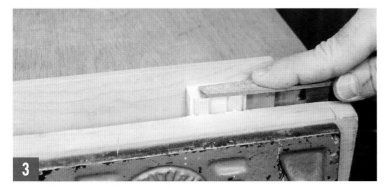

**3** **File or sand the ends flush with the** truck frame.

**4** **Determine the hitch spacer thickness.** Place the trailer behind the truck on a flat surface. Measure the gap above the truck frame and the trailer deck. This should be close to ⅛ in. Make the spacer. It is ¾ x ¾ in. by the thickness needed to fill the measured gap (about ⅛ in. thick).

**5** **Sand the edges smooth and glue the** spacer in place. The spacer is ⅝ in. from the front edge of the trailer deck.

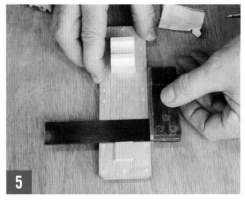

**6** Mark out hole locations. If holding in a vise, be sure to put a spacer in the dowel side to avoid pressing them out when tightening the vise.

**7** Set up to drill the axle holes. Use a vise or use a square block of wood as an angle bracket, with a wood scrap spacer to account for the dowel posts. Check that the trailer is level and the drill bit is parallel to the deck. Drill the axle holes to $\frac{5}{32}$ in. for the $\frac{1}{8}$ in. dowel axles.

## HITCH

**1** Drill for the hitch dowel (see page 19). Stop about $\frac{1}{16}$ to $\frac{1}{8}$ in. before breaking through.

**2** Cut a short piece of dowel. Mark a cut line with the dowel in place and bevel the end so that it is easier to hitch the trailer to the truck. Put glue in the hitch hole and insert the hitch dowel.

## COMPLETING

See page 23 for finishing information, and pages 10 to 21 for wheel information.

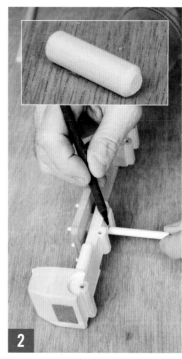

# DEUCE COUPE

This toy is modeled after the classic 30s Ford Deuce Coupe, which is still a very popular die-cast toy. It is an easy build (our wooden toy, not the original hot rod) consisting of a single small block of hardwood, and then four wheels of your choice. Rev your engine and get ready to cruise around town in style!

## CUT LIST

| NO. REQ'D | PART NAME | MATERIAL | T" | W" | L" | NOTES |
|---|---|---|---|---|---|---|
| 1 | Body | Hardwood | 1⅛ | 1¼ | 3 | Rough-cut oversize (see instructions). |
| 1 | Front axle housing | 5/16 in. dia. dowel | | | 1 | |
| 2 | Front wheels | ⅝ in. dia. factory-made contour | | | | See pages 10 to 21 for custom wheel choices. |
| 4 | Rear wheels | ¾ in. dia. factory-made contour | | | | Glue into two pairs. See instructions. |
| 2 | Axles | ⅛ in. dia. dowel | | | To fit. | |

*Note: Dimensions are finished sizes. Most parts should be rough-cut oversize. See instructions.*

## ASSEMBLY GUIDE

**Top**

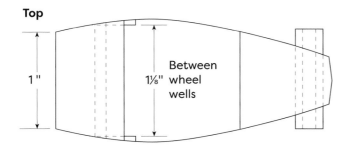

1 "

Between
1⅛" wheel
wells

1⅛" H x 1¼" W x 3" L

**Side**

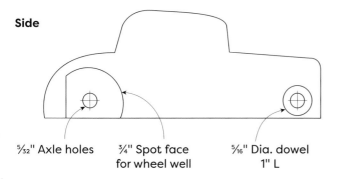

⁵⁄₃₂" Axle holes     ¾" Spot face
for wheel well     ⁵⁄₁₆" Dia. dowel
1" L

## TEMPLATES

**Top**

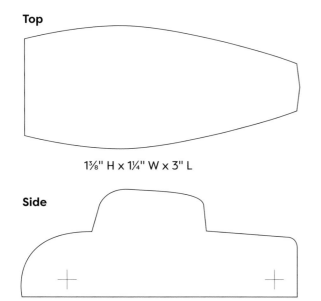

1⅜" H x 1¼" W x 3" L

**Side**

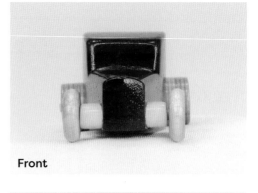

Front

Back

Side

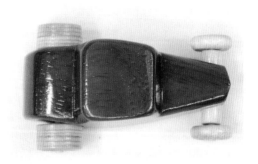

Top

# CAR

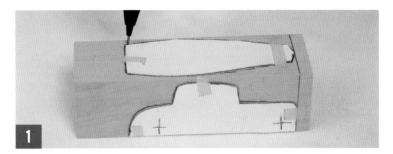

**1** **Prepare a block of wood at least** 3¼ in. long by 1¼ in. wide by 1¼ in. thick. Glue and clamp pieces together if needed. Mark a line for the car front slightly in from one end, using a square to continue it around the block. This allows template alignment on the top and sides. Mark out the profiles on the top and sides. Mark the axle holes with an awl on both sides.

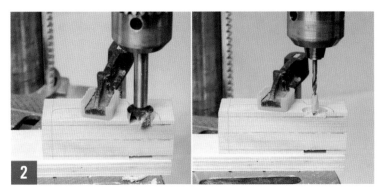

**2** **Drill the shallow wheel well recesses** for the rear wheels with a ⅞ in. Forstner bit. The distance between the bottoms of these holes will be 1 in.; mark the depth on the bottom surface (if your block is exactly 1¼ in. wide, the depth will be ⅛ in.). Drill one wheel well; without moving the part, change to a ⁹⁄₆₄ or ⁵⁄₃₂ in. drill bit. Drill the axle hole a little over halfway through.

**3** **Turn the car block over and do the** same on the other side. Then, drill the ⁵⁄₁₆ in. hole for the front axle housing dowel. This hole should come close to the bottom of the car, but still leave ¹⁄₃₂ to ¹⁄₁₆ in. of wood. Drill this hole slowly and carefully.

**4** **Partially cut the top profile, but leave** at least ¾ in. uncut in the roof area so that no pieces are actually removed yet. You will want the sides attached when placing the car on its side to cut the side profile. Leave the car about ¹⁄₁₆ in. overlong at the front grille.

**5** Place the car on its side and saw out the side profile.

**6** Now go back and finish off the top profile cuts by eye. You could sketch in the lines to join the gaps, if that seems necessary. File and sand to remove the saw marks and to smooth the curves. At the front, smooth the grille angles but leave the edges at least $\frac{1}{32}$ in. and up to $\frac{1}{16}$ in. from the front axle holes.

**7** File and sand to shape the radius that rounds the hood. Start by filing angles on each side. While shaping the hood, you end up shaping the bottom edge of the windshield, so do this as you go along, being careful to keep a clean transition between the two. It is easy to undercut one or the other. If this happens, file the other surface to smooth them out. The exact angles and radii are not critical, just aim for smooth lines and symmetry side to side.

**8** Round out the roof and the trunk (rumble seat) area. The trunk is rounded above and behind the wheels, with about a $\frac{1}{16}$ in. radius. The roof has slightly smaller rounds, but is domed a little. Finish sanding the sides of the hood where the dowel axle housing will go.

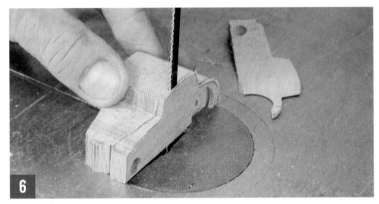

# FRONT AXLE HOUSING

**PROJECT NOTES**

This axle housing is drilled before it is glued into the car body. It could also be drilled after it is glued in, as is done with the 1930s sprint car (page 98). However, the deuce coupe is more difficult to line up exactly square to the drill press table. If it is drilled inaccurately, that would be hard to repair, so follow the steps carefully.

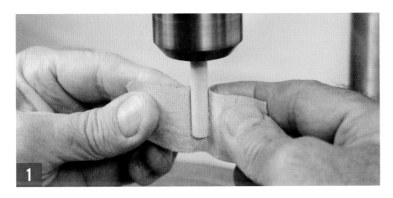

**1** **Check that the axle dowel slides easily** (but not loosely) into the front axle hole. If it is tight it may crack the car body when tapped into place, so sand it to fit. Cut the dowel an inch too long, then chuck it in the drill press. When it is spinning, it can be sanded with fine-grit sandpaper. When the dowel axle housing is a good sliding fit, cut it to 1¹⁄₁₆ in. length and mark the center of each end.

**2** **Drill the ⁵⁄₃₂ in. axle hole through the** center of the axle housing. You have a few setup options for this tricky step. If you have a wood lathe with a chuck, use that. Otherwise, clamp the dowel in the drill press so that it is vertical. A vise that has a vertical "V" groove is best.

Another holding option is a squared-up block of wood with a vertical saw kerf.

A third option is a squared-up block of wood with a vertical wood strip glued on.

**3** **Use a toothpick to apply glue in the** hole and on the outside of the dowel in the area that will remain inside the car. Insert the dowel. Check that the dowel is centered. Before the glue is fully hardened, remove any excess from the dowel ends with a small chisel or razor knife, then sand smooth.

## COMPLETING

See page 23 for finishing information, and pages 10 to 21 for wheel information.

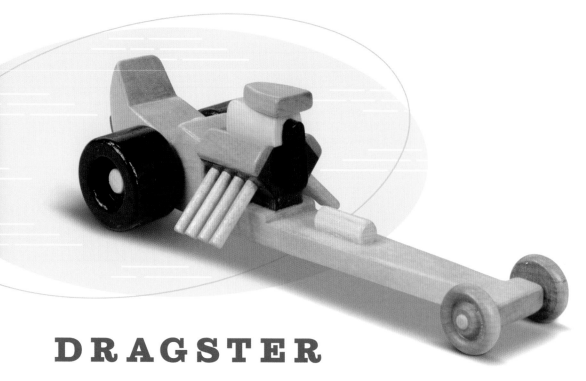

# DRAGSTER

In this toy, the engine is of an extreme size, almost entirely blocking the driver's view. A few front engine rails were like this, although many had a design that allowed for slightly better visibility. The engine takes the most time to make—probably more than the rest of the car. It consists of several small parts, but these details make it easily identifiable as a gas-gobbling racing engine.

**Front**

**Back**

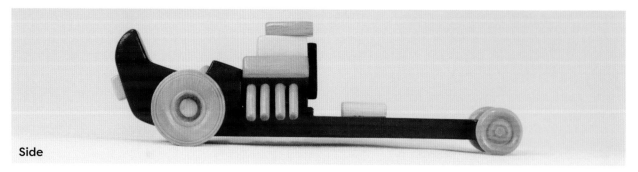

**Side**

## CUT LIST

| NO. REQ'D | PART NAME | MATERIAL | T" | W" | L" | NOTES |
|---|---|---|---|---|---|---|
| 1 | Engine block | Hardwood | ⅝ | ⅞ | ⅞ | See instructions for rough length. |
| 1 | Oil pan | Hardwood | ⅛ | ⅜ | ⅞ | Only needed if making engine block with tablesaw. Rough-cut ½₂ to ¹⁄₁₆ in. overlong. |
| 2 | Valve covers | Hardwood | ⅛ | ¼ | ⅞ | |
| 1 | Supercharger | Hardwood | ¼ | ⅜ | ¾ | |
| 1 | Intake scoop | Hardwood | ⅛ or ³⁄₁₆ | ½ | ⅝ | |
| 1 | Drive belt | Hardwood | ⅛ | ¼ | ¾ | |
| 8 | Exhaust pipes | ⅛ in. dowel | | | ⅞ | Length to suit. See instructions. |
| 1 | Frame | Hardwood | ¾ | 1½ | 5½ | |
| 1 | Steering wheel | ⅜ in. dowel | | | ⅛ | See instructions for rough length. |
| 1 | Fuel tank | ¼ in. dowel | | | ⅝ | |
| 1 | Chute | Hardwood | ⅛ | ⅜ | ⅜ | |
| 2 | Front wheels | Factory-made ⅝ in. dia. contour | | | | See pages 10 to 21 for custom wheel options. |
| 2 | Rear slicks | Factory-made 1 in. dia. treaded | | | | See pages 10 to 21 for custom wheel options. |

*Note: Dimensions are finished sizes. Most parts should be rough-cut oversize. See instructions.*

## TEMPLATES

**Dragster body**
¾" H x 1½" W x 5½" Lg

**Body Nose**

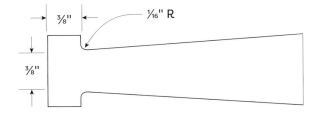

⅜"  ¹⁄₁₆" R  ⅜"

Body Side

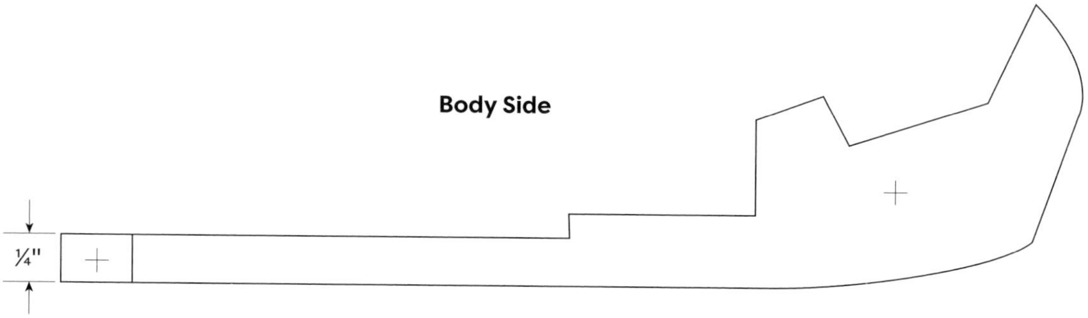
1/4"

## ASSEMBLY GUIDE

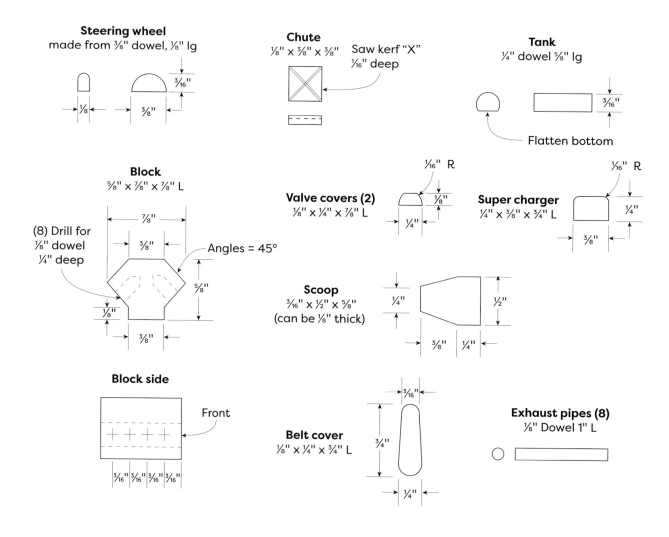

**Steering wheel**
made from 3/8" dowel, 1/8" lg

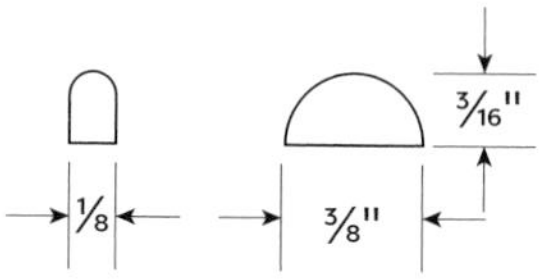
3/16"
1/8
3/8"

**Chute**
1/8" x 3/8" x 3/8"

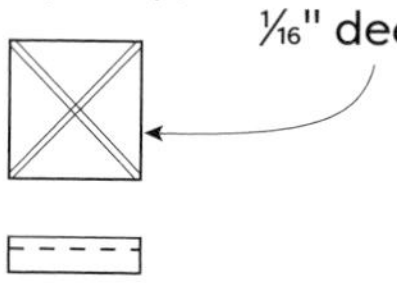
Saw kerf "X"
1/16" deep

**Tank**
1/4" dowel 5/8" lg

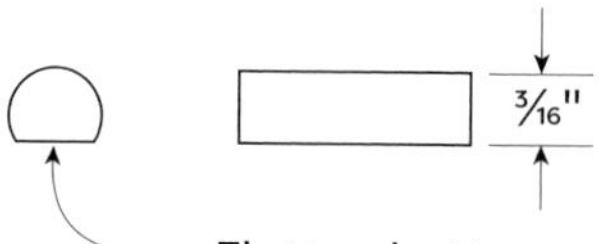
3/16"
Flatten bottom

**Block**
5/8" x 7/8" x 7/8" L

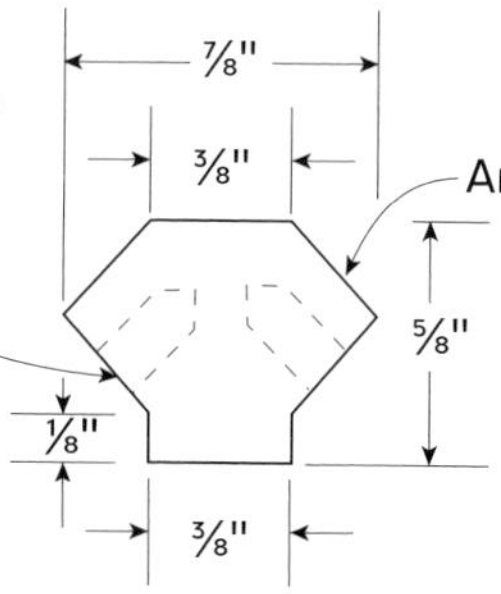
7/8"
3/8"
(8) Drill for
1/8" dowel
1/4" deep
Angles = 45°
5/8"
1/8"
3/8"

**Valve covers (2)**
1/8" x 1/4" x 7/8" L

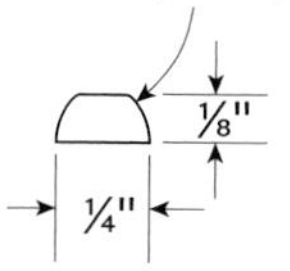
1/16" R
1/8"
1/4"

**Super charger**
1/4" x 3/8" x 3/4" L

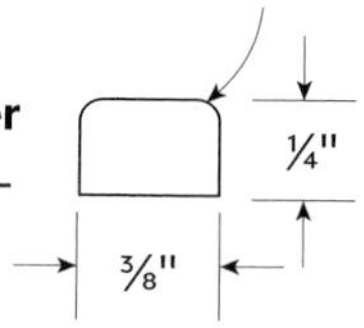
1/16" R
1/4"
3/8"

**Scoop**
3/16" x 1/2" x 5/8"
(can be 1/8" thick)

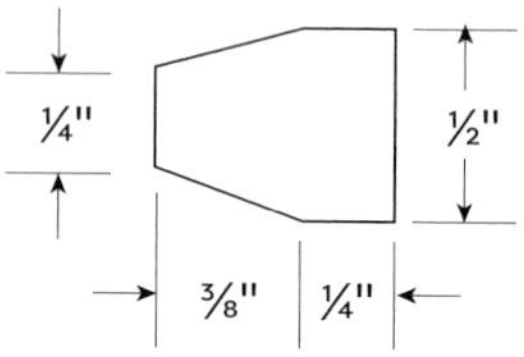
1/4"
1/2"
3/8"
1/4"

**Block side**

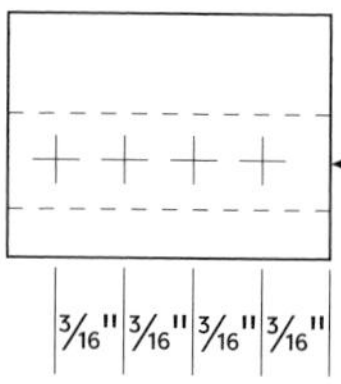
Front
3/16" 3/16" 3/16" 3/16"

**Belt cover**
1/8" x 1/4" x 3/4" L

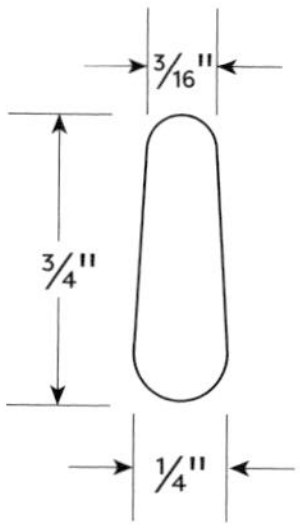
3/16"
3/4"
1/4"

**Exhaust pipes (8)**
1/8" Dowel 1" L

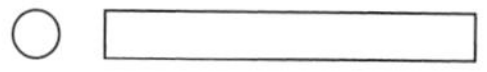

# ENGINE BLOCK

## TABLESAW METHOD

For the Bandsaw Method, see page 68.

**1 Select a wood strip to form the heads** and top of the engine block. To safely cut the angles with a tablesaw, you need a long strip, about 12 x ½ x ⅞ in. Saw the first two 45° angles. Set the fence to allow the saw blade to enter the wood halfway up (¼ in. above the table). This will be very close to a ⅞ in. gap from the fence to a 90° saw blade. Cut the angle, then flip the wood upside down and cut the other half of that edge.

**2 Reset the saw fence. The flat on the** top should be ⅜ in. or just over. The fence should now be set ⅟₁₆ in. narrower, or very close to ¹³⁄₁₆ in. Saw the second two 45° angles. Saw off the ⅞ in. length.

**3 Saw the oil pan piece. It is ⅜ in. wide** (to match the flat engine block bottom) by ⅛ in. thick, and as long as the engine block plus ⅟₃₂ in. Sand the saw marks out.

**4 Glue the oil pan to the engine block.** Press the parts in place by hand, or use a clamp if needed to close any gaps.

Go to Drilling on page 68.

## BANDSAW METHOD

**1** **Cut a slice from a board end so when** the engine block is cut, the grain will run lengthwise. This allows good glue surfaces for added engine parts. Shown is purpleheart, roughly ⅞ in. thick by 4 in. wide. Cut a slice ¹⁵⁄₁₆ to 1 in. long (this will be the length of the engine block). Use the template or measure out the end profile. Position it so the top of engine block is on a straightedge.

**2** **Saw the 45° angles but leave the** engine block attached to the larger board for now. Machine-sand the angles. Keep the angled surfaces flat, especially where the valve covers are attached later (page 69).

**3** **Saw off the engine block from the** larger wood piece.

# DRILLING

**1** **Mark out the exhaust pipe holes. These** run down the center of the two angled surfaces, ³⁄₁₆ in. apart, starting ³⁄₁₆ in. from one end (the engine front). The last hole center is ⅛ in. from the back end. Make indents with an awl. Choose a drill bit to fit your ⅛ in. dowels (see page 19). Set up the engine block in the drill press. Use a vise or parallel clamp (Jorgensen type), gripping the engine block ends. Keep the angled surface parallel to the drill press table, so the drill is at 90°. Do the same on the other side.

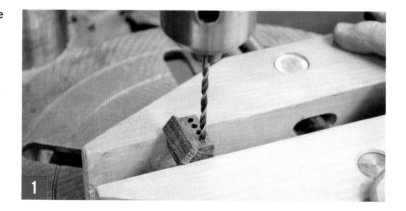

## VALVE COVERS

**1** Measure the size of the two valve covers. They will be about ¼ in. wide, but can be adjusted for a good fit to suit the block. Mark the length to be about ¹⁄₃₂ in. longer than the engine block. Yellowheart contrasts with the dark engine block.

**2** Cut the valve covers ¹⁄₃₂ in. longer than the block. Sand to remove saw marks and to break the corners.

**3** Glue the valve covers to the engine. Press them firmly into place for a minute or so, then let the glue harden.

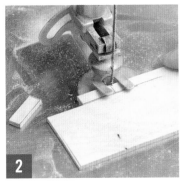

## SUPERCHARGER

**1** Cut the supercharger block. Use ¼ in.-thick stock, ¾ in. long by about ⅜ in. wide (to fit the top of the engine block, between the valve covers). Consider a light-colored wood because these superchargers are often chromed. Sand to remove saw marks and to round the top sides. Remove all sharp corners except around the base, where it will be glued to the engine.

**2** Glue the supercharger to the block. Minimize squeeze-out; it is hard to remove from the small space between the supercharger and valve cover. Overhang the front of the supercharger off the block about ¹⁄₃₂ in. Clamp if needed, but likely pressing into place will work. Sand the front and back of the engine assembly flush with a sanding board. Hand-sand to break all the sharp corners except on the bottom of the oil pan, which is the glue surface to the dragster frame.

## INTAKE SCOOP

**1** Mark out the scoop contour on a piece of ⅛ in.-thick wood. Shown is yellowheart, to match the valve covers. Saw the scoop to size. As always with tiny parts, plan your cuts so they are made while the wood is large enough to keep your fingers clear of the blade.

**2** Sand to remove saw marks and round over all the sharp corners, then glue to the supercharger. Have the scoop centered and protruding over the front of the engine slightly (about ¹⁄₁₆ in.).

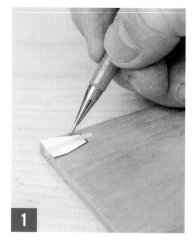

## DRIVE BELT

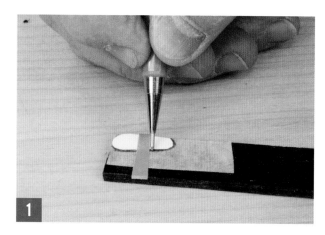

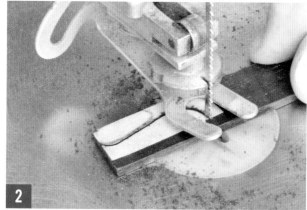

**1** Mark out the supercharger drive belt. Use ⅛ in.-thick wood. An actual belt is black, so choose a dark wood. Apply masking tape for easier viewing of the lines.

**2** Saw to the lines. Leave it attached to the larger piece until the sanding is done.

**3** File or sand to round the corners. Remove saw marks and sharp edges except on the glue surface, where the belt will attach to the block.

**4** Saw to remove the belt from the larger wood piece. Finish sand. Glue the belt to the engine. Have it centered side to side, and with about a 1/16 in. gap between the belt top and the underside of the scoop.

## EXHAUST PIPES

**1** Cut the exhaust pipes from 1/8 in. dowel. The pipes should extend about 5/8 in. from the block, so measure the depth of holes and cut the dowels accordingly. Dowels will be sanded even after assembly, so they can be 1/16 in. too long now. Bevel one end slightly so it will enter the drilled holes easily, then put a little glue into the holes with a toothpick. Press into place. Dowels might be at slight angles to each other; move them around to align.

**2** Even up the ends of the dowels. When all the glue is dry, sand or saw the ends even. Hand-sand around the ends to break the sharp corners.

**3** The engine is now complete.

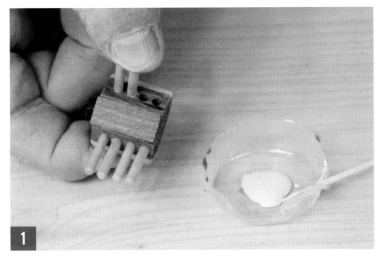

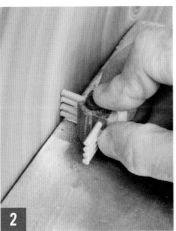

# FRAME

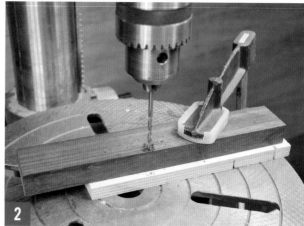

**1** Mark out the frame. Use a piece of ¾ in.-thick hardwood. Trace the template and mark the axle hole locations with an awl.

**2** Drill the front axle hole. A %₆₄ or ⁵⁄₃₂ in. drill bit will allow the ⅛ in. axle to spin freely (see page 19).

**3** Drill the rear axle hole. A ⁹⁄₃₂ in. drill bit provides clearance for the ¼ in. axle.

**4** Saw the frame profile.

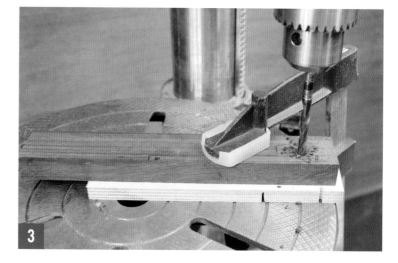

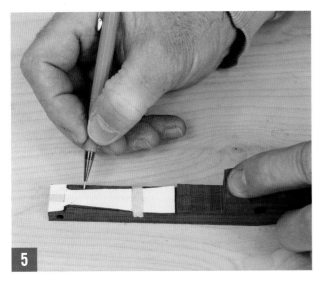

**5** Mark out the taper on the front half of the frame. The frame narrows down to ⅜ in. just behind the front axle housing. The axle housing section should be ⅜ in. wide as well.

**6** Saw the angled surfaces. File and sand them smooth. Sand to break the sharp corners and edges.

**7** File and sand the profile. Take care to keep the engine mount surface and the chute mount surface (lower rear straight section) as flat as possible.

**8** Disc-sand the cockpit area. Starting at the rear axle hole, the sides should taper back to about ½ in. wide at the rear. Sand to smooth and remove all sharp corners.

## STEERING WHEEL

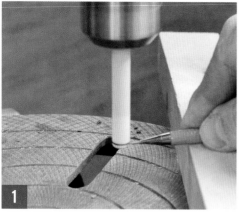

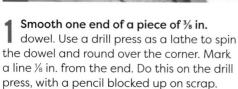

**1** Smooth one end of a piece of ⅜ in. dowel. Use a drill press as a lathe to spin the dowel and round over the corner. Mark a line ⅛ in. from the end. Do this on the drill press, with a pencil blocked up on scrap.

**2** Partially saw to ⅛ in. length. Stop just over halfway through.

**3** Saw to remove the half circle of the steering wheel. A little over half is fine also.

**4** Glue the wheel to the dashboard. You may need to round over the straight edge if there is a slight radius in the corner of the dashboard. Press it into place by hand.

## FUEL TANK

**1** Cut the ¼ in. dowel. Sand one end to smooth and remove sharp corners; cut the ½ in. length; then sand the other end. File or sand a small flat (⅛ in. to 3/16 in. wide) for a glue surface. Glue the tank in place in front of the engine with about a ½ in. gap between the end of the tank and the engine mount section of the frame.

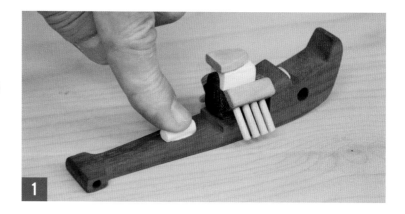

# CHUTE

**1** **Cut the small strip of light-colored** wood to contrast with the darker wood of the frame. It is ⅜ in. wide by ⅛ in. thick by at least a couple inches long. Mark the outlines. Draw a line ⅜ in. from the end, and mark out an "X" to represent the straps.

**2** **Saw the "X" grooves. Use a saw or** corner of a file to "engrave" the lines and make them visible.

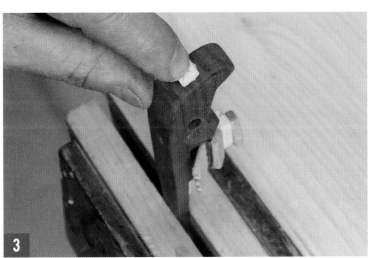

**3** **Saw to length. Sand to smooth the** ends and round the sharp corners. Glue the chute to the rear flat section of the frame. Keep it centered and toward the top of the flat.

## COMPLETING

See page 23 for finishing information, and pages 10 to 21 for wheel information.

The photos of this project show standard factory-made 1 in. diameter treaded wheels for the slicks, and ⅝ in. diameter contour wheels for the front. If you wish, you could make slightly wider slicks, using a dark wood strip ⅝ in. thick, and drilling out wheels using a 1¼ in. diameter hole saw.

# MONSTER TRUCKS × 3

Monster truck toys were in production almost as soon as the first Bigfoot 4x4 truck made its debut in 1979. The popularity of monster truck shows and toys has grown steadily since then. Two main body styles are shown: a pickup truck modeled after the Ford truck of Northern Nightmare; and a panel truck modeled after Grave Digger. The panel truck has an option for front fenders and an angled windshield, which is a third variation. Get ready to crush the competition with your choice of big tires (see page 16).

## CUT LIST

| NO. REQ'D | PART NAME | MATERIAL | T" | W" | L" | NOTES |
|---|---|---|---|---|---|---|
| 1 | Pickup or panel truck body | Hardwood | 1 ¼ | 1 ½ | 3 ¼ | |
| 1 | Panel body with front fenders (optional) | Hardwood | 1 ¼ | 1 ½ | 3 ¼ | Rough length is 3 ¾ in. |
| 2 | Veneer fenders (optional) | Veneer | ⅟₆₄ to ⅟₃₂ total | 1 ½ | 2 ¼ | Rough-cut the veneer to at least 2 ¼ in. square. |
| 1 | Frame | Hardwood | ¾ | 1 | 3 ¼ | |
| 8 | Wheels | Factory-made 1 ¼ in. dia. treaded | | | | Glued together to make four wide wheels. See pages 10 to 21 for custom wheel instructions. |
| 2 | Axles | ¼ in. dowel | | | To fit. | |

*Note: Dimensions are finished sizes. Most parts should be rough-cut oversize. See instructions.*

## MONSTER PANEL TRUCK

Front

Back

Side

Top

## MONSTER PANEL TRUCK WITH FENDERS

Front

Back

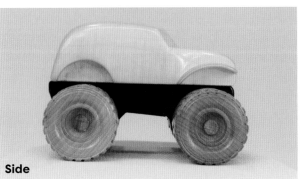

Side

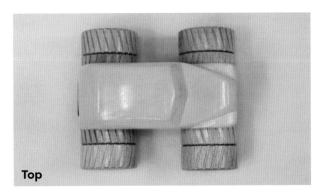

Top

## MONSTER PICKUP TRUCK

**Front**

**Back**

**Side**

**Top**

## TEMPLATES

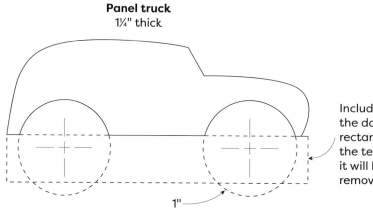

**Panel truck**
1¼" thick

Include the dashed rectangle in the template; it will be removed later.

1"

**Panel with fenders**
Rough: 1¼" T x 3¾" L

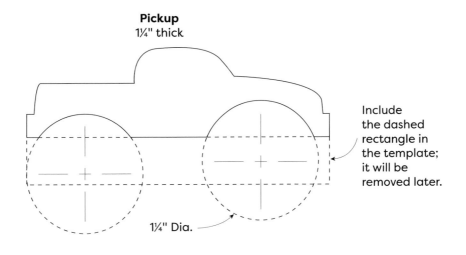

Include
the dashed
rectangle in
the template;
it will be
removed later.

**Pickup**
1¼" thick

Include
the dashed
rectangle in
the template;
it will be
removed later.

1¼" Dia.

**Frame**
¾" thick

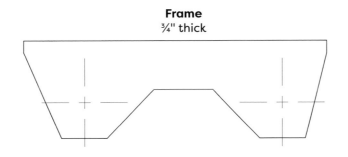

# PICKUP TRUCK BODY

**1** **Make a block of wood at least 3¾ in.** long by at least 1½ in. wide (to make drilling wheel wells easier before final sizing) by 1¼ in. thick. On the 1½ in. side, use the template to mark out the side profile and an awl to mark the centers for the wheel wells. If using dark wood, apply masking tape to allow visibility of pencil lines. Use a square to carry the centerlines over, then measure the same distance up from the edge of the block and mark the centers on the other side as well.

**2** **Drill the wheel wells. Use a** 1 in.-diameter Forstner-style drill bit, and drill ¼ in. deep (side-to-side distance between the wheel wells should end up at ¾ in. or slightly smaller to match the frame width). Clamp the body to the drill press table securely and set a depth stop, or mark the drill bit with masking tape.

**3** **Saw the profile. Now that the wheel** wells are drilled, saw the outline of the truck body. Saw the bottom surface as well.

**4** **Round all sharp corners. The radius will** be about ⅟₁₆ in. Exact size is not critical; round the corners until you are happy with the general look. Sand the bottom surface flat. Move ahead to making the frame, page 86.

# PANEL TRUCK BODY & FENDERS

To make the panel truck without veneer fenders, use the template on page 78, but follow the pickup truck body instructions on page 80.

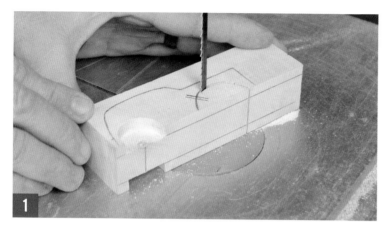

## BODY

**1** To make this panel truck with veneer fenders, use the template on page 79, then follow the monster pickup truck page 80 steps 1 and 2, but only drill out the rear wheel wells. For the front wheel wells, saw to the line carefully with a small bandsaw blade (maximum ¼ in. blade): one cut only; no relief cuts. You will need the off-cut later to clamp the veneer in place and then glue it back into place under the veneer fenders. Mark the front wheel well off-cut so you know which way it goes back in later. If the cut is rough, sand the largest of the ridges off, being careful to keep the cut lines square so the off-cut will fit well when glued back in later. Depending on the veneer thickness, you may need to sand a little extra to allow a good glue fit later.

## VENEER FENDERS

**1** Cut three pieces of thin hardwood veneer, 1½ in. wide by at least 2¼ in. long. They can be rough-cut to at least 1¾ by 2¼ in. rectangles. Two pieces have grain crosswise to the truck body, with one piece having lengthwise grain. The combined thickness of the veneer should be the same as the saw kerf of the blade used to cut the wheel well.

**2** Soak veneers for 20 minutes. Make a very simple veneer-bending fixture by tracing the fender curve from the template and cutting it out from scrap. This will allow you to bend the wet veneer without getting the truck parts wet. Have cross-grain veneer on top and bottom, and the lengthwise veneer sandwiched between. Set it aside to dry for a couple hours at least.

**3** Glue the veneer together. When dry, the veneers can be glued to each other but not to the wheel well yet. Use a small piece of plastic on each side of the veneer fender to make sure the veneer doesn't adhere to the truck body. Have the veneer centered side to side within ⅛ in. or so, and protruding out each end slightly (at least ⅛ in.).

**4** When the glue is dry, remove the fender lamination. Mark the veneered fender so you will know which way it goes back in later.

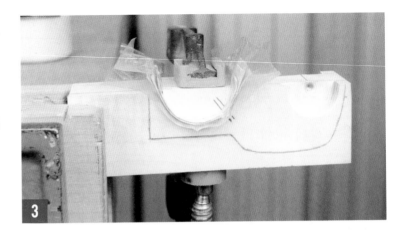

## PROFILES & SHAPING

**1** Saw to square off the hood top surface.

**2** Saw the side angles of the hood area. Mark the front edge 3¼ in. back from the back of the truck. Mark the side angles; the width of the hood is ½ in. at the front and full width at the windshield line. Leave the hood top rough, but file and sand the hood sides.

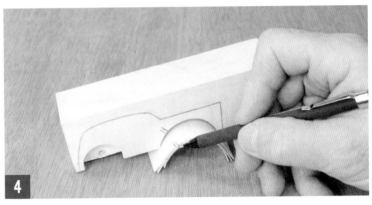

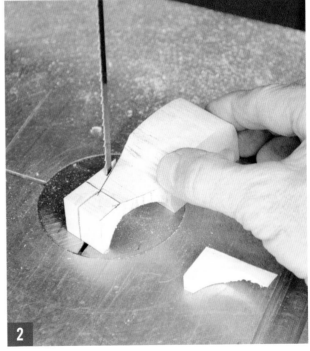

**3** Glue the laminated fender into its location under the hood. Temporarily use the fender cut-off to help clamp the fender into place.When the glue is dry, sand the sides flush with the truck. Sawing sometimes leaves splinters, so sanding is preferable.

**4** Saw the bottom fender surfaces flush.

**5** Mark the ¾ in. width of the wheel well off-cut. With scraps, place a carpenter's pencil above the table to align with the original ¾ in.-wide lines; then move the off-cut around to mark out the curved surface. Saw the off-cut to ¾ in. width. This can be up to ¹⁄₃₂ in. narrower, but shouldn't be wider or it may contact the wheels later. Clamp the small part to keep the cut more accurate and safer.

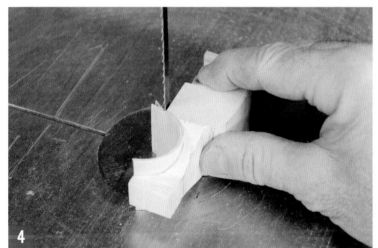

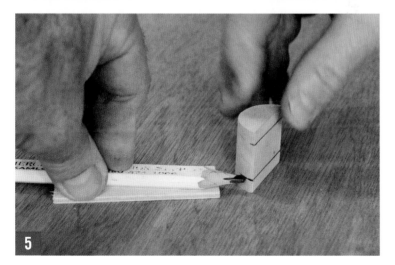

**6** Glue the wheel well off-cut back in place. Sand the sides to remove saw marks and carefully center it side to side. Mark out the bottom cut line. This will be ¼ in. up from the current bottom. Use the template to check if in doubt.

**7** Mark out the grille area cut. This will make the truck 3¼ in. long. Saw the bottom. Saw the front.

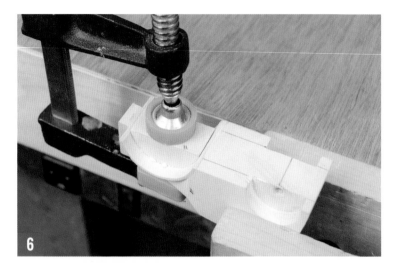

## HOOD & WINDSHIELD

**1** Mark out the hood and windshield profiles. The windshield is measured back ⅛ in. at the corners. The hood curve starts ½ in. from the front, and curves down to a thickness of ⅜ in. up from the bottom of the body.

**2** Shape the hood curve. Saw and file, or disc sand.

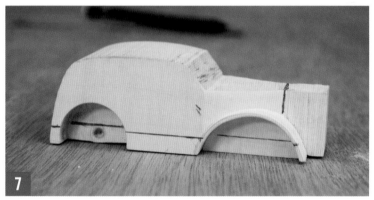

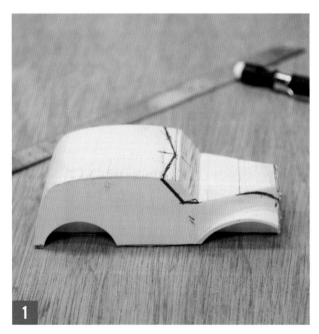

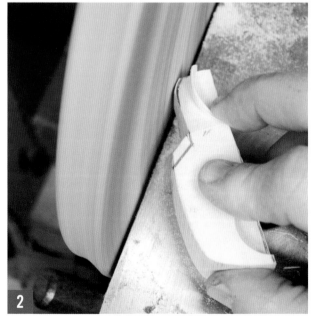

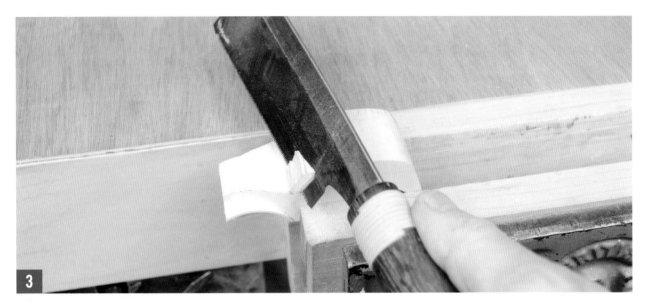

**3** Saw the windshield angles. A small handsaw is shown.

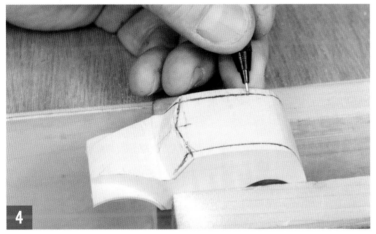

**4** Mark out the side window angles. These are in about ⅛ in. at the top, and angled down to the bottom of the windshield corners.

**5** Sand the side window angles. A wedge similar to the off-cut left over from the tractor wheels fixture (page 18) or the boat fixture (page 105) is helpful to guide the sanding. Saw the bottom of the truck to the line. This will make the fender off-cut, the fender excess, and the truck body all flush and flat. Round all sharp corners to about ⅛ in. radius. Proceed to make the frame.

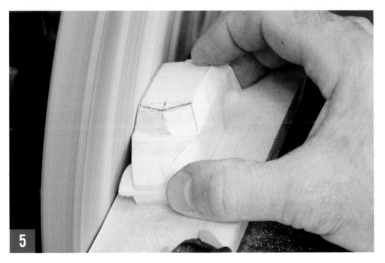

# FRAME

**1** **The frame is a block of wood at least** 3¼ in. long by 1 in. wide by ¾ in. thick. As with the body, cut a longer strip to allow safe tablesaw use, and to make more than one frame. Mark out the profile. Locate the axle center holes with an awl. The top surface of the frame should be a machined flat surface. Drill the %₃₂ in. axle holes. Clamp the frame to the drill press table and drill through. Saw the frame to shape. Sand or file to remove saw marks. Keep the top of the frame flat for a good contact with the bottom of the body.

**2** **Glue the frame to the body. Center** the frame side to side, using the wheel wells as location references, and add glue. Clamp lightly in a vise, or if needed, with a vise and clamp.

# WHEELS

There are several choices. See the section on making wheels, pages 10 to 21. You could saw out approximately 1¼ in. wheels using a 1⅜ in. or 1½ in. hole saw, then sand the periphery smooth to remove the saw cuts; or try one of these options.

# COMPLETING

See page 23 for finishing information.

Factory treaded wheels with cross cuts give a knobby off-road look.

Tractor tires look good too.

The simplest choice is to use 1¼ in. diameter factory-made wheels, either treaded or flat.

# SCHOOL BUS

This is one bus that you'll never miss! The interior seats are a fun option and not hard to add. However, the bus looks great without the interior detail. If you expect very young children to play with this bus, skip the interior. This will ensure that no little fingers get caught in the window openings. Choose a yellow wood to make this project even better.

## CUT LIST

| NO. REQ'D | PART NAME | MATERIAL | T" | W" | L" | NOTES |
|---|---|---|---|---|---|---|
| 1 | Body interior | Hardwood | 1 ½ | 2 ¼ | 5 ½ | |
| 2 | Body sides | Hardwood | ⅛ | 2 ¼ | 5 ½ | |
| 6 | Wheels | Factory-made ¾ in. contour | | | | Optional custom wheels; see pages 10 to 21. |
| 4 | Flasher lights (optional) | Hardwood or ¼ in. dowel | | | | See instructions. |

*Note: Dimensions are finished sizes. Most parts should be rough-cut oversize. See instructions.*

Side

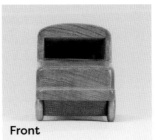
Front

Back

## TEMPLATES

**Bus interior**
1½" × 2¼" × 5½"

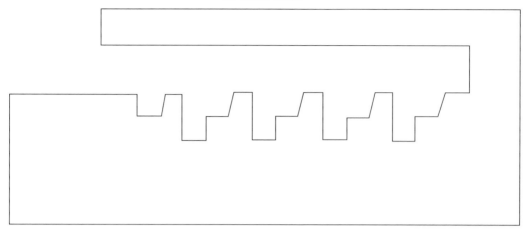

**Bus side (2)**
⅛" × 2¼" × 5½"

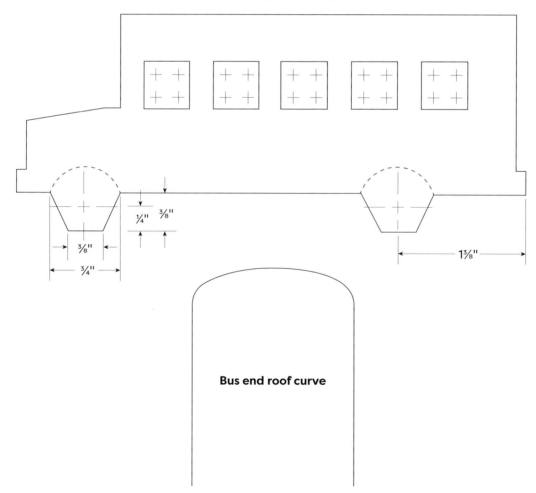

Bus end roof curve

# BODY INTERIOR

**1** **You may need to laminate a block,** as shown. The bus should be about 1¾ in. thick when assembled. Shown is a block 1½ in. thick for the interior with two ⅛ in.-thick sides. If using ¼ in.-thick sides, the interior block should be only 1¼ in. thick. Either way, it will be at least 5½ in. long by at least 2¼ in. wide. Mark out the optional interior contour with the template or measure it. Saw the interior contours to form the seating.

**2** **Smooth the seats and ceiling.** Use a fine-tooth small file and minimal sanding to remove sharp corners. Round the top and ends of the seat backs slightly; this area will be seen later.

**3** **Spray-finish the interior.** Mask off the sides of the bus, leaving the seat area exposed, then apply the finish.

# SIDES

**1** **Use the same color wood as the interior** block. Sides should be at least 2¼ in. wide by at least 6 in. long for now, by ⅛ in. thick (could be up to a maximum of ¼ in. thick, if the interior body block is reduced to 1¼ in. thick). Prepare the template, if using. Mark the contour on one piece. Locate the template so that you have a bit of excess on each end for now (to allow for temporary glue spots).

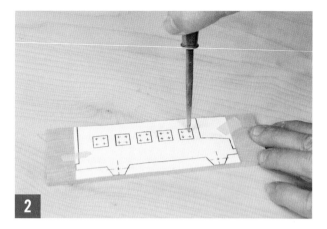

**2** **Mark the axle and window hole** centers. Each window has a hole in the corner to make sawing easier. If you don't have a 1 in. flat-bottom bit, use a compass now to draw the ½ in. radius wheel wells. They can be sawn out instead, but you won't have dual wheels in the back. The window layout should be clear and accurate, so to ensure alignment, go over the lines with a straightedge and a square.

**3** **Temporarily glue the two sides** together. Dab a bit of glue in the corners, on spots that will be removed when the sides are cut out. Tape the bottom side. Masking tape will reduce the amount of chip-out on the underside when sawing.

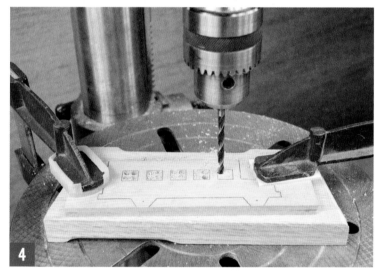

**4** **Drill the window corner holes. The** centers are located ⅛ in. from the window edges, but instead of using a ¼ in. drill bit, try a ³⁄₁₆ or ⁷⁄₃₂ in., which allows a tiny bit of clearance from the window edge. Saw very carefully along the lines. Accurate cutting here will reduce the amount of filing and sanding needed later.

**5** **First file or sand a small bevel on the** corners of the window openings to reduce splintering, then use a small file to remove the sawing marks. As you file, check the window alignment. The tops and bottoms of the windows should be aligned as closely as possible. Check with a straightedge, or redraw straight lines to help check. Saw the outside contour. This will separate the two sides. Remove the sharp edges around the windows. Sand both sides of the window openings.

# ASSEMBLY

If you are making the basic bus (no interior cutouts), you may want to darken the area that will be behind the window openings to give the idea of depth. If so, mask off the sides so only the window areas are stained.

**1** **Glue one side in place. Apply glue all** around the perimeter, but be sparing near the window openings to avoid glue squeeze-out. Glue the second side in place. Line up the two sides as carefully as possible. Have the axles directly across from each other (draw a line with a square). When the glue is dry, sand the bottom flat and square to the sides. This will allow you to use a square for accurate wheel center layout next. Also sand the top flush.

**2** **Mark out the axle centers on the** second side. Carry the centerline across the bottom and up the unmarked side. Measure up from the bottom to match the first side layout. It is important for this to be accurate as possible or the wheels will look off-center later.

**3** **Saw the outside contour. This needs to** be done before the wheel well drilling removes the axle housing outline.

**4** **Drill out the wheel wells. The front** wheel well depth is ⅛ to ⁵⁄₃₂ in. (about the thickness of the wheel), and the rear is double that if using dual wheels.

**5** Drill the axle holes. These should be about ⅟₃₂ in. larger than the axle size. For the sample, there are ⅛ in. holes in the ⅝ in.-diameter contour wheels, so ⁵⁄₃₂ in. holes are shown. Use a high RPM and a low feed rate to keep the drill bit from "wandering" as it drills this relatively deep hole. Clear the chips often.

**6** File and sand the outside contour. Start with a machine sander where possible; bevel the corners slightly so they don't chip, then file out the saw marks using a small smooth file or sandpaper. Leave final sanding until after the optional light holes are drilled.

**7** Mark out the roof arc. Use the template or mark it out by eye on the front and rear of the bus.

**8** Rough out the radius. Machine-sand or handplane the roof. Exact radius isn't critical, but keep it symmetrical side to side as much as possible. File and sand to round over about a ⅛ in. radius in the hood and grille area, and about ⅟₁₆ in. radius around the bottom and back.

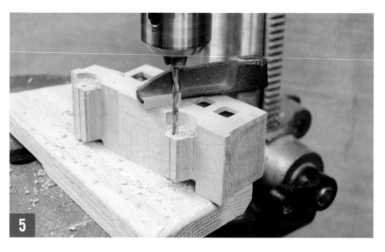

5

6

7

8

# LIGHTS (OPTIONAL)

**1** **If desired, make red flasher lights.** These fit best on the basic bus. You can use a ¼ in. plug cutter with red wood, such as padauk, or use a maple dowel and dye it red with food coloring. If using a dowel, it's easier to round the end before cutting to length. In the photos, the lights are ¼ in. diameter, and the holes are about ¼ in. down from the top and ⅜ in. in from the edges, but the location isn't critical. Drill the holes.

**2** **Glue the lights into place. Put a tiny bit** of glue into the holes, and push or tap the lights into place. If using dowels, saw the lights to length before gluing (see next step). They should protrude between 1⁄32 in. and 1⁄16 in.

**3** **Sand to remove sharp corners. Sand** the lights to smooth the saw cuts, and to slightly round the sharp corners. This has already been done if using dowels.

## COMPLETING

See page 23 for finishing information, and pages 10 to 21 for wheel information.

As shown, this bus uses ¾ in.- diameter factory-made contour wheels with ⅛ in. holes and axles. You could use the same wheels that have 3⁄16 in. holes and axles, if that is what you have.

# 1930S SPRINT CAR

These small and stylish cars were made by Ferrari, Maserati, and others back in the early days of racing. Very soon the die-cast toy companies were selling their versions. This wooden model has a one piece body, with two solid axles and factory-made contour wheels. Grab your driving goggles, gloves, and scarf and hit the track in style!

## CUT LIST

| NO. REQ'D | PART NAME | MATERIAL | T" | W" | L" | NOTES |
|---|---|---|---|---|---|---|
| 1 | Body | Hardwood | ¾ | ¾ | 3 | |
| 2 | Axle housings | ⁵⁄₁₆ in. dowel | | | 1 ¹⁄₁₆ | |
| 1 | Steering wheel (optional) | ⁵⁄₁₆ or ⅜ in. dowel | | | ⅛ | Cut after rounding. See instructions. |
| 4 | Wheels | Factory-made ⅝ in. dia. contour | | | | For custom wheel options, see pages 10 to 21. |

*Note: Dimensions are finished sizes. Most parts should be rough-cut oversize. See instructions.*

Front

Back

Side

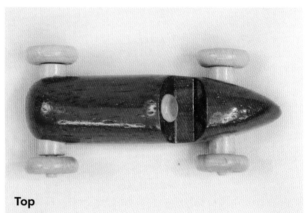

Top

## ASSEMBLY GUIDE & TEMPLATES

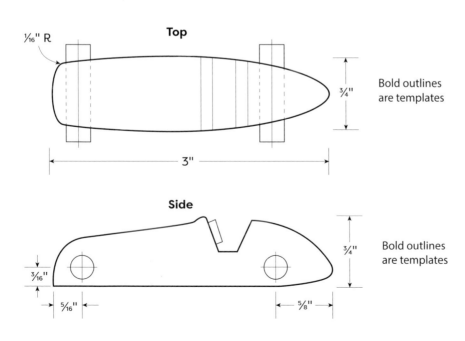

Top

¹⁄₁₆" R

Bold outlines
are templates

³⁄₄"

3"

Side

Bold outlines
are templates

³⁄₄"

³⁄₁₆"

⁵⁄₁₆"

⁵⁄₈"

## BODY

**1** **You'll need a rectangular block at least** ¾ in. thick by at least 3 in. long. Width is not too important yet, but it will end up close to ¾ in. Use the templates for the top and side contours. Leave a little extra material below the "floor" of the car body; you'll trim it to size after the axle holes are drilled. Mark out the axle housing hole locations and drill the holes to fit a ⁵⁄₁₆ in. dowel (see page 19).

**2** **Start the saw cuts. Saw the sides at** the rear end, but leave the last bit uncut so the side contour can be cut to shape easily. It is a good idea to hold the block with a clamp to keep fingers a comfortable distance from the blade.

**3** **Saw the side contours. Leave about** ¹⁄₃₂ in. for sanding.

**4** Finish the saw cuts. Go back and finish the cuts to form the pointed rear part.

**5** Disc-sand or file the sawn surfaces to the lines. The exact shape is not critical, but the curves should be smooth and symmetrical.

**6** Smooth the car body. Plane, file, and sand to round over sharp edges. Radii in the drawings are approximate, but should be smooth and symmetrical. The hood is more rounded than the rear. There is a small lip where the windshield would be. Use a fine round file (a chainsaw tooth file works) to carefully create a small radius there. It is a bit fiddly, so if you can't get it to work, just get rid of the small lip. Finish sanding. Remove all file and saw marks.

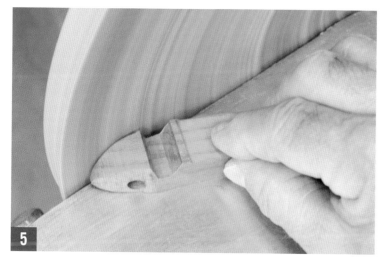

## AXLE HOUSINGS

**1** **Cut the axle housings to 1¹⁄₁₆ in. long.**
They should slide into the car body easily, but not rattle. Smear a bit of glue on the center where the housing will contact the body. Keep the ends clean; this will save cleaning later. Slide into place, checking they are centered with a ruler. The axle housing is about ¹⁄₁₆ in. too long at this point, so you have that much leeway.

**2** **When the glue is dry or almost dry,** carefully scrape off any excess. Place a short piece of ½ in. dowel in the driver's seat to allow the vise to grip the car without damaging it. Trim the housing ends. Check that the housings are centered on the body. If not, file or sand the longer ends until it is all even, or at least within ¹⁄₃₂ in. Pencil a dot on each center end of the axle housings. It is okay to do this by eye; it seems to be just as accurate as measuring on these tiny surfaces. Use a sharp awl to make a dimple.

**3** **Drill the axle holes. The axle dowel is** ⅛ in. diameter, so drill the holes ⁹⁄₆₄ in. Clamp the car to a block of wood with a short piece of dowel in the seat area. Place a scrap of plywood under the car. Drill each side so the holes meet in the middle. If they are not exactly aligned, you can open them up with a ⁵⁄₃₂ in. bit to ensure the axle spins freely.

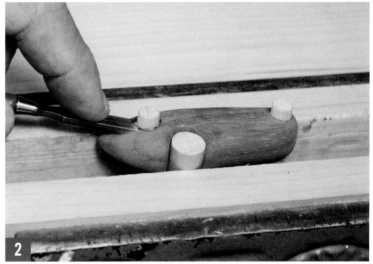

# STEERING WHEEL (OPTIONAL)

**1** **Select a short length of ⁵⁄₁₆ or ⅜ in.** dowel. Chuck it in the drill press with about ¾ in. protruding, and sand the cut end to smooth it and round the sharp corner slightly. Use the corner of a file to make a groove about ³⁄₃₂ or ⅛ in. from the end. Sand to remove the file marks.

**2** **Saw the steering wheel from the dowel.**

**3** **Glue the steering wheel into place.** You may need to flatten the cut edge by carefully rubbing it on a piece of sandpaper. Put a dab of glue on the rougher side and hold it with finger pressure for a minute, then set aside to harden.

## COMPLETING

See page 23 for finishing information, and pages 10 to 21 for wheel information.

# SEA

Zoom from beach to beach with these water-dwelling toys. Sail the seven seas by boat or turn the water into your very own runway with the float plane!

# COAST GUARD BOAT

This boat is modeled after the 40-foot utility boat used by the Coast Guard. The toy is meant to be carried by the flat deck trailer (page 54), pulled by the cab-over truck (page 47). The hull may be made from one solid block, or may be laminated from several. A strip of darker wood can be used to approximate the paint stripe seen on some Coast Guard boats. Skip over the waves and get ready to defend the coastline!

## CUT LIST

| NO. REQ'D | PART NAME | MATERIAL | T" | W" | L" | NOTES |
|---|---|---|---|---|---|---|
| 1 | Hull | Hardwood | 1 | 1 ¾ | 5 ¼ | Can be laminated if a colored stripe is desired. See instructions. |
| 1 | Wheelhouse | Contrasting hardwood | ¾ | 1 | 2 | |
| 1 | Deck winch | ¼ in. dia. dowel | | | ½ | |
| 2 | Stern and bow lights (optional) | ⅛ in. dowel | | | ½ | |
| 1 | Wheelhouse lights (optional) | ⅛ in. dowel | | | ½ | |
| 1 | Wheelhouse horn (optional) | ⅛ in. dowel | | | ⅜ | |
| 1 | Fuel container (optional) | ¼ in. dowel | | | ½ | |

*Note: Dimensions are finished sizes. Most parts should be rough-cut oversize. See instructions.*

Front

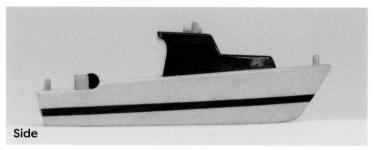
Side

Back

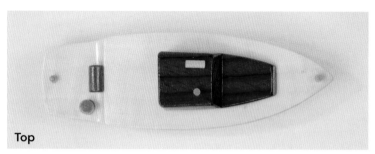
Top

## ASSEMBLY GUIDE

**Top**

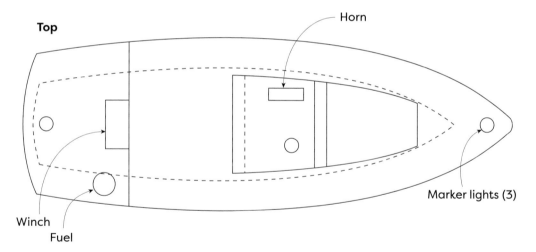

Horn

Marker lights (3)

Winch

Fuel

**Side**

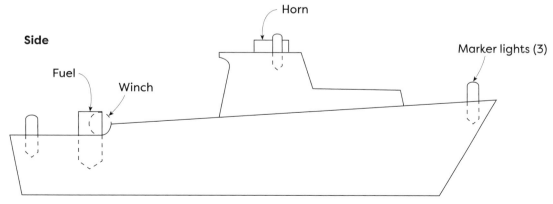

Horn

Marker lights (3)

Fuel

Winch

## TEMPLATES

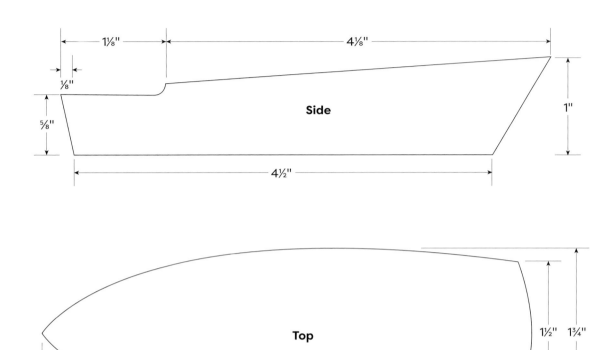

Side

Top

Wheelhouse top

Wheelhouse side

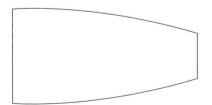

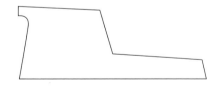

# HULL

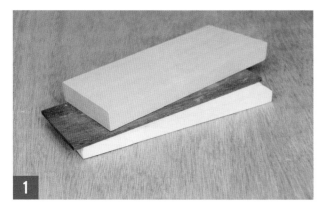

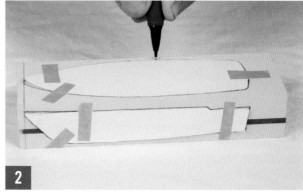

**1** **If not laminating, cut the wood block** at least 5¼ in. long by at least 2 in. wide by at least 1 in. thick. For the color stripe version, cut three pieces. The top piece shown is ¾ in.-thick maple, the bottom is ⅜ in.-thick maple, and the color stripe is ⅛ in.-thick padauk. Glue the laminations together. When the glue is dry, plane or belt-sand the sides flat and square to allow layout and sawing.

**2** **Trace the side and top profile outlines.** Use the template and line the side profile up using the strip as the reference. As shown, the template is oriented so the color stripe is lower at the stern and rising toward the bow.

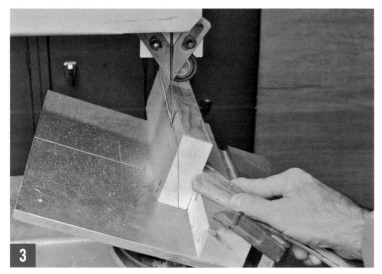

**3** **Make a simple angle fixture to cut** the angled sides of the hull. If your bandsaw table tilts both ways, you can skip this step. For the majority of bandsaws that tilt only one way, saw a 20° surface on a 2 x 4 to make a reversible fixture. Keep the off-cut angled board as well; it will be smaller and works on the disc sander to smooth the saw cut later.

**4** **Space the fixture off the table with** ¾ in. plywood scraps. This allows the boat hull to rotate around on the fixture without contacting the table. Saw and stop about ½ in. from the middle of the hull. This will allow you to cut the side profile before completing the cut. You will be able to cut from the front (bow) on one side and the stern on the other side before reversing the fixture.

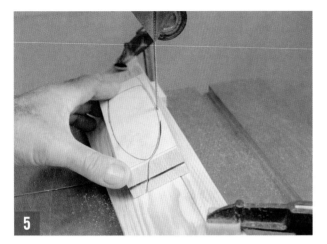

**5** Reverse the angle fixture and make two more cuts. Leave at least ½ in. uncut on each side.

**6** Saw the curve that forms the stern or transom.

**7** Saw the top (deck) surface and the bottom (hull) surface, then use the angle fixture again to finish the cuts that form the hull sides. Hand-sand or disc-sand to remove the saw marks from the sides.

**8** Sand the slight angle on the stern. The exact angle is not at all critical. Smooth the deck and bottom surfaces. A sanding board works well. Keep the deck surface flat, so it will form a good glue joint when the wheelhouse is attached.

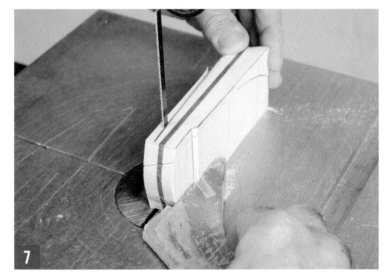

# WHEELHOUSE

**PROJECT NOTES**

The wheelhouse is only 2 in. long, but you should start with a block 6 in. or more in length to make it easier (and safer) to handle.

**1** **The block should be at least 2 in. long** by at least 1 in. wide by at least ¾ in. thick, but 6 or 8 in. long makes it much easier to handle. The bottom needs to be exactly flat to provide a good glue surface. Mark out the top and side contours with the templates. Place the wheelhouse bottom on the machined-flat surface of the block, and the front of the wheelhouse at the end of the wood strip.

**2** **Partially saw the angled rear surface.** Leave the roof overhang attached to the longer block for now. Take a couple of cuts to roughly form the radius under the overhang. Partially saw the windshield notch. Leave at least ⅛ in. uncut so the top profile can still be seen. Leave the roof top for now if your block is only ¾ in. thick; you will cut or sand the slight roof slope later.

**3** Saw the slightly rounded sides.

**4** Finish the windshield cut.

**5** **Trim the roof angle. This slope will allow** the roof to be horizontal when the wheelhouse is attached to the slope of the deck. File and sand to smooth the sides and windshield notch.

**6** Angle the sidelights. Mark out the slight angles on the sides of wheelhouse, then file or sand these small surfaces. Smooth the top, sides, and front of the wheelhouse, and break all sharp corners. Leave the bottom unsanded so it stays flat.

**7** Saw to remove the wheelhouse. File and sand the rear surfaces under the overhang.

**8** Glue the wheelhouse to the deck. Center it side to side and set back about 1 in. from the bow so that the side curves of the wheelhouse approximately match the side curves of the hull. It does not need to be clamped if it sits flat on the deck. When the glue is partially hardened to a rubbery state, scrape off the excess. Finish-sand the hull.

# FINISHING TOUCHES (OPTIONAL)

**PROJECT NOTES**

These simple options make the boat look a bit more interesting.

**1** Mark out the hole locations. All holes are ¼ in. in from the edge. Stern and prow holes are centered side to side. Drill holes about ¼ in. deep, using a stop or tape to mark the depth.

**2** Cut the vertical dowel pieces. Round or angle the ends somewhat before cutting them off the dowel. For rounded ends, finish the end on the drill press by chucking the dowel in the drill, then sand while spinning the dowel in the machine (see page 20). Cut to length. They should protrude from the surface between ⅛ and ¼ in.

**3** Glue the dowels in place. Put a small amount of glue in each hole using a toothpick, then press the dowels in.

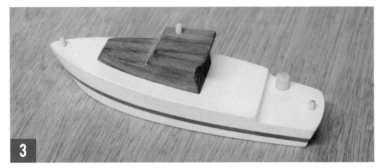

**4** Flatten one side of the horizontal dowel (horn) to provide a glue surface. Glue the horn in place by putting a thin string of glue on the flat using a toothpick, then press it into place and leave it to dry.

## STERN DECK WINCH

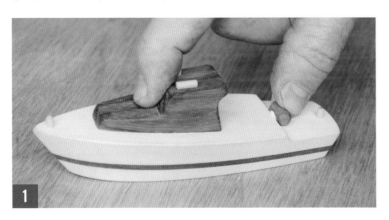

**1** Cut the ¼ in. dowel to ½ in. length. Exact diameter and length are not critical. Shown is a piece of walnut dowel, but other colors are fine too. Sand to smooth the ends and round the sharp corners, then glue into place.

## FINISHING

See page 23 for finishing information.

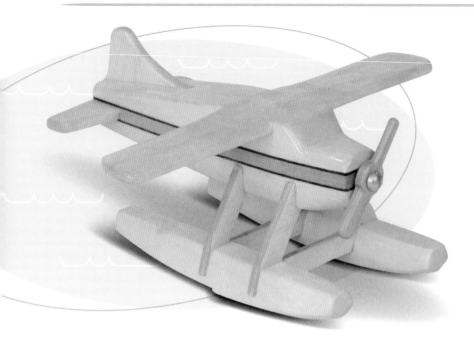

# FLOAT PLANE

This float plane is modeled after the legendary Beaver bush plane. Of the toys in this book, this is likely the most time consuming to make. However, each part on its own is quite manageable and the result is a great little toy. Fly up to your forested cabin and land on the lake for a nice vacation!

## CUT LIST

| NO. REQ'D | PART NAME | MATERIAL | T" | W" | L" | NOTES |
|---|---|---|---|---|---|---|
| 1 | Fuselage | Hardwood | ¾ | ⅞ | 4 | Can be laminated if a colored stripe is desired. See instructions. Rough length should be 8 to 12 in. |
| 2 | Floats | Hardwood | ½ | ½ | 3 ¼ | Cut oversize; see instructions. |
| 1 | Vertical stabilizer (tail) | Hardwood | ⅛ | 1 ¼ | 1 ½ | Cut oversize; see instructions. |
| 1 | Horizontal stabilizer (rear wing) | Hardwood | ⅛ | ½ | 2 | |
| 2 | Float struts | Plywood | ⅛ | 1 | 2 | |
| 1 | Propeller | Hardwood | ⅛ | ⁵⁄₁₆ | 1 ¼ | |

*Note: Dimensions are finished sizes. Most parts should be rough-cut oversize. See instructions.*

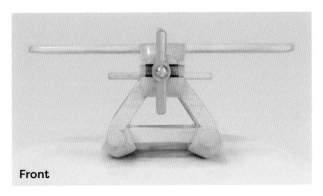

Front

Back

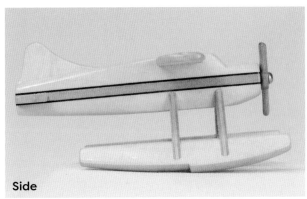

Side

Top

## TEMPLATES

**Side**

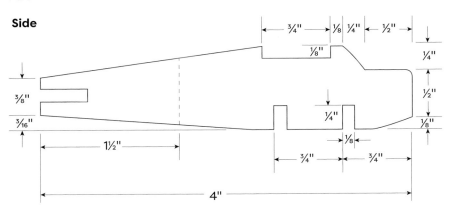

**Propeller**
Drill to fit woodscrew

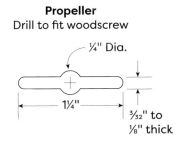

¼" Dia.

1¼"

³⁄₃₂" to
⅛" thick

**Top**

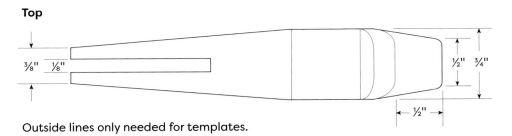

Outside lines only needed for templates.

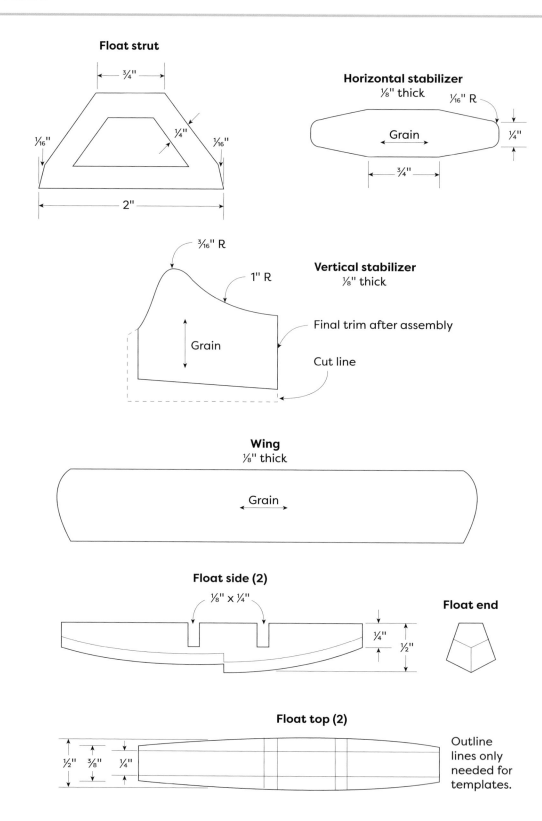

**Float strut**

¾"

¼"

¹⁄₁₆"  ¹⁄₁₆"

2"

**Horizontal stabilizer**
⅛" thick

¹⁄₁₆" R

Grain

¼"

¾"

³⁄₁₆" R

1" R

**Vertical stabilizer**
⅛" thick

Grain

Final trim after assembly

Cut line

**Wing**
⅛" thick

Grain

**Float side (2)**

⅛" × ¼"

¼"  ½"

**Float end**

**Float top (2)**

½"  ⅜"  ¼"

Outline
lines only
needed for
templates.

# FUSELAGE & FLOATS

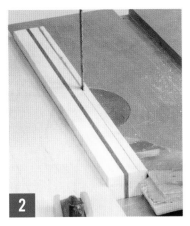

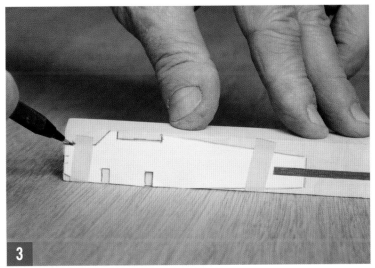

**1** **Make the fuselage block 8 to 12 in. long** by 1 in. wide by at least ¾ in. thick. You could make the fuselage from a single block of wood, if desired. If laminating, glue and clamp: the maple bottom strip is at least ¼ in. thick, the top maple strip is at least ½ in., and the middle is a ⅛ in. strip of padauk. When the glue is dry, smooth the thin strip flush with the wider pieces.

**2** **Trim the cut the fuselage block to** size—¾ in. wide and ⅞ in. high—paying attention to the location of the ⅛ in. strip. It should be about ⅜ in. from the center of the thin strip to the bottom of the fuselage. Most of these surfaces will be angled and rounded later, but leave it rectangular until the dadoes are cut.

Rough out the wood for the float blocks to 8 to 12 in. long (to make the dadoes easier to cut) by 1¼ in. wide by ½ in. thick.

**3** **Use the templates or measure to mark** out dado locations on the floats and fuselage, as well as the side profile of the fuselage. On the fuselage, have the ⅛ in. strip centered to the propeller center at the front, and to the rear wing location at the tail end.

**4** **Carry the dado locations across the** top of the floats and up the side of the fuselage so the two parts can be lined up for dado cutting.

**5** **Make a test cut to check width of the** ⅛ in. dado with ⅛ in. tablesaw blade and Baltic birch plywood. You can sand the plywood a bit if needed to fit the dado, or add in a thin piece of veneer if the plywood is too thin.

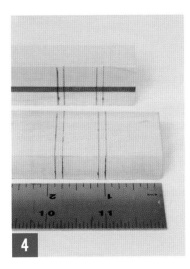

**6** Cut the dadoes in the fuselage and floats. Tape the three parts together to allow cutting of the dadoes on floats and fuselage all at the same time.

**7** Saw the wing dado. Take the three blocks apart; cut the 1/8 in. deep by 3/4 in. wide dado for the wing. Later, you can size the wing width to be an exact fit in the dado. Make seven or eight cuts with the regular 1/8 in.-thick blade.

**8** Saw the tail dado. Cut the fuselage to length, then cut the vertical stabilizer (tail) dado, 1/8 in. wide by 1 1/2 in. deep. Clamp the small piece to the miter gauge as shown (a plywood fence is shown attached to the miter gauge). Center it, check it for square, then make the cut.

**9** Mark out the side contour using the template. Saw out the contours of the top side of the fuselage (cockpit and tail section), but leave the fuselage bottom for now. Leave a little (1/32 in.) for filing and sanding to the lines. File and rough-sand to the lines.

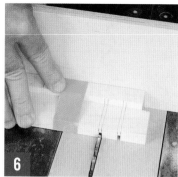

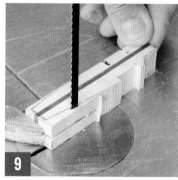

# TAIL (VERTICAL STABILIZER)

**1** Lay out the tail contours. Use 1/8 in.-thick hardwood with the grain running vertically. (You may want to mark out the wings and propeller too). Saw to size and shape, leaving about 1/32 in. for final sizing and sanding.

**2** Put glue into the 1/8 in. tail dado and a small amount onto the tail itself. Clamp lightly. When the excess glue is partially hardened, carefully remove it with a small chisel or scraper.

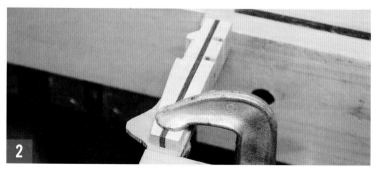

**3** When the glue is completely dry, trim and sand the bottom and back end surfaces flush, and blend the top front surface into the top fuselage surface.

**4** Cut the ⅛ in. rear wing (horizontal stabilizer) dado in the fuselage, ½ in. deep. Clamp the fuselage to the miter gauge and center the cut to the ⅛ in. strip.

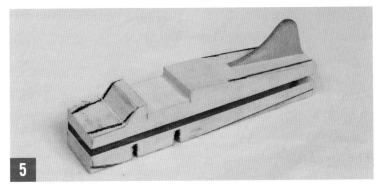

**5** Mark out the angles on the bottom and sides of the fuselage. Saw the bottom tapers. These are at the front and back of the fuselage. A clamp allows a safer grip and better control of the cut. Rotate the piece and saw the slight angles on the sides of the fuselage.

**6** Round all the corners, particularly in the front cowl area and toward the tail. Exact radius isn't critical; shown is between ¹⁄₁₆ and ⅛ in. on the fuselage, and slightly more at the engine cowling area. At the front, the cowling will be round or close to it. Use a small file for this. Finish-sand the fuselage.

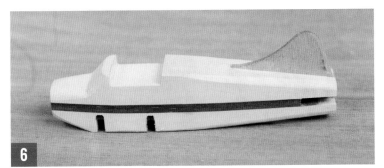

# WINGS

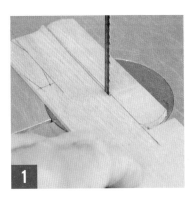

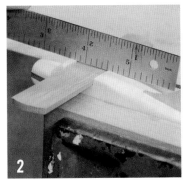

**1** Mark out and saw the wing and horizontal stabilizer. The wing should be very slightly wider (¹⁄₃₂ in.) than the wing dado at this point.

**2** Fit the wing into the dado by planing or sanding to a snug fit. The dado needs to fit the thickness of the wing. If the dado is too deep, remove the excess wood from the fuselage now. It is okay if the wing protrudes a little (i.e., the dado is slightly too shallow).

**3** Draw small lines when the wing is centered on the fuselage. These lines will make assembly easier, and will allow you to slightly shape the wing cross section while leaving this center part rectangular.

**4** Finish shaping and sanding the wing and the horizontal stabilizer now. Round all the corners and edges of the horizontal stabilizer until smooth and safe. You can do the same with the wing, or give it the semblance of an aerodynamic profile— the top surface a little more blunt at the leading edge, and tapering off at the trailing edge.

## FUSELAGE & WING ASSEMBLY

**1** Glue the wings into place. Put glue into the rear dado, but only a little on the rear wing (horizontal stabilizer). Glue the main wing to the dado on the top of the fuselage. Check that it is centered. If it is loose, add a piece of veneer under the wing. Trim the veneer to exact size after the glue is dry. When the glue is dry, finish-sand the joint area to blend wing into fuselage.

## FLOATS

**1** Find the block of wood for the floats (with the two small dadoes cut along with the fuselage). Cut into two strips, each about ½ x ½ in., but leave the parts full length (8 to 12 in. long).

**2** Mark out the top and side profiles. Draw the lines that outline the top final width ¼ in. apart.

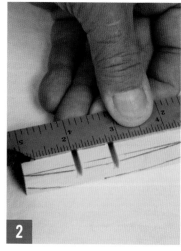

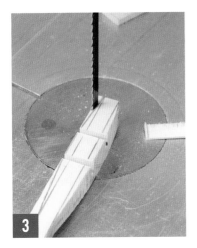

**3** Cut the bottom and then the side surfaces. Carry the cuts along for about an extra ½ in. or so. Leave the float attached to the longer block. Sand or file the surfaces to remove most of the saw marks.

**4** Draw a centerline on the bottom surface. A flexible straightedge is handy.

**5** File (or sand) the "V" shape of the hull. It is about 20°.

**6** File the side angles. Leave the top of the float ¼ in. wide as marked out in step 2. This will leave the front and rear ends of the float looking unfinished, so these will need to be narrowed slightly to blend the angles. Finish-sand the floats. Saw the floats to length. Sand the cut end smooth. Break the sharp corners with sandpaper.

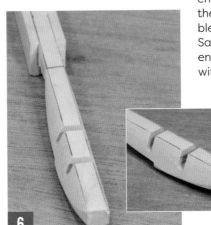

## FLOAT STRUTS

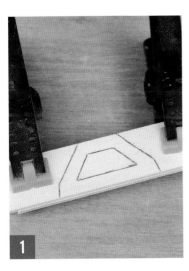

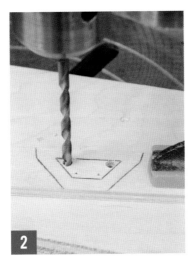

**1** Cut two strips of 1 in.-wide ⅛ in. Baltic birch plywood a little longer than needed. Lay out the outline on one of the pieces. Use small dabs of glue at each end to glue the two strips together. When the ends are sawn off, the struts will separate.

**2** Birch plywood tends to splinter, so it is a good idea to attach a piece of tape to the underside before drilling and sawing. Drill holes in the corners to allow the blade to be inserted.

**3** Use a scroll saw or coping saw to remove the interior. File to smooth the sawn surfaces, except the top interior surface (this happens after the struts are glued to the fuselage, see step 5). To reduce chipping out, file or sand a small bevel (1⁄32 in.) on the back edges before smoothing the sawn surfaces to the lines. Saw the outside contour, leaving about 1⁄32 in.

**4** Check that the strut fits the fuselage. If needed, mark and sand off any excess so the strut blends into the fuselage.

**5** Glue the struts to the fuselage. It is simplest to clamp it gently in a vise. When the glue has started to harden, remove the excess. Smooth the strut interior to be flush with the fuselage. Glue the floats to the struts. The struts should protrude slightly (1⁄64 to 1⁄32 in.) outside the floats. Clamp the parts gently and let dry. Smooth the struts so they are flush with the float sides.

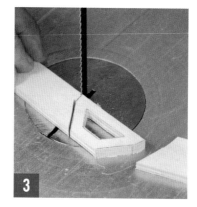
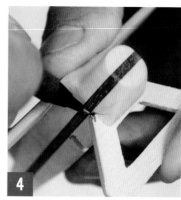

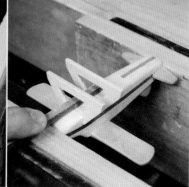

# PROPELLER

Brass screws are weak and can break in a finished toy, so it pays to be careful and drill a test hole in a scrap of the same wood you're using for the plane and try the screw in that scrap. As seen here, the first hole on the right is too small and the screw broke. It is also a good idea to drill very slightly larger if using a brass screw instead of a steel one.

**1** Mark the center of the nose for the propeller mount screw. Determine the correct pilot bit size for the propeller-mount screw. Shown is a #5 screw with a recommended bit size of 5⁄64 in. to 3⁄32 in. A #40 drill bit works here, which is only .005 in. larger than 3⁄32 in., but does reduce the chances of breakage.

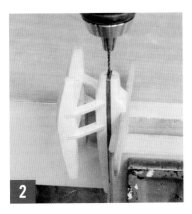

**2** Drill the hole. The plane is difficult to hold in a drill press at this point, so carefully drill using a hand drill. Check that the plane and drill bit are both vertical. This doesn't have to be perfect, but should be close.

**3** Mark out the propeller screw hole. Use a piece of ⅛ in. thick hardwood. Have the hole about ¼ in. from the edge for now, and at least ⅝ in. from the end of the wood. Because the part is so small and drill bits can wander, drill the hole first and mark out the propeller outline after. Drill the screw hole. It should be large enough for the screw threads to fit through, with only a little clearance.

**4** Mark out the propeller outline. With the blades being ⅛ in. wide, and the hole ⅛ in. also, it is easy to mark the parallel lines just tangent to the hole. Saw to the lines, leaving a very small amount for filing. Use a clamp if needed to keep fingers away from the blade. A scroll saw is also a good option. File to the lines with a small and inexpensive jeweler's file.

**5** Saw the blades to length and round the ends. Sand to round any sharp corners.

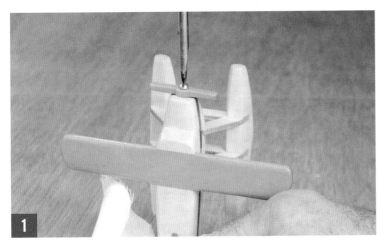

# FINISHING

**1** Spray a clear gloss finish onto the plane and the propeller before assembly. This tends to keep the propeller spinning more freely later, and makes it a bit easier to finish the nose of the plane. After the finish has completely hardened, screw the propeller to the fuselage. Some paraffin wax on the inside surface of the propeller where it contacts the plane keeps the freshly finished surfaces from sticking. A little on the screw itself reduces the chance of breakage. See notes on finishing, page 23.

# AIR

This high-flying quartet with real spinning propellers will put your head in the clouds. With iconic fighter jets and even a helicopter to choose from, you'll never want to come down to earth!

# CORSAIR FIGHTER PLANE

The Vought F4U Corsair fighter plane was made for many years, from the 1940s to the 60s. It had a reputation as an excellent plane, and had a distinctive profile, complete with "W" wings. These things also made it a very popular die-cast toy from the 50s through today. This toy version has a solid wood fuselage, with a layered veneer wing. Zip through the air, and don't forget to do loop-de-loops!

## CUT LIST

| NO. REQ'D | PART NAME | MATERIAL | T" | W" | L" | NOTES |
|---|---|---|---|---|---|---|
| 4 to 8 | Wing veneers | Veneer (total thickness ³⁄₁₆ in.) | ³⁄₁₆ | 1¼ | 6¼ | Cut veneer oversize. Alternate grain directions. See instructions. |
| 1 | Horizontal stabilizer (rear wing) | Veneer (total thickness ⅛ in.) or ⅛ in. hardwood | ⅛ | ¾ | 2½ | Cut veneer oversize. Alternate grain directions. See instructions. |
| 1 | Vertical stabilizer (tail) | Veneer (total thickness ⅛ in.) or ⅛ in. hardwood | ⅛ | 1¼ | 1½ | As above, or if using solid wood, note grain direction. See instructions. |
| 1 | Fuselage | Hardwood | ¾ | 1 | 5 | |
| 3 to 5 | Propeller veneer | Veneer (total thickness ⅛ in.) | ¹⁄₆₄ to ¹⁄₃₂ | 1½ | 1½ | Cut veneer oversize. Alternate grain directions. See instructions. |
| 1 | Fuselage, lower section | Hardwood | ⁵⁄₁₆ | ¾ | 6⅜ | Rough-cut about 12 in. long if possible. See instructions. |

*Note: Depending on the thickness of the veneer, you will likely need between 1 and 2 square feet of veneer to make all the required parts for this toy.*

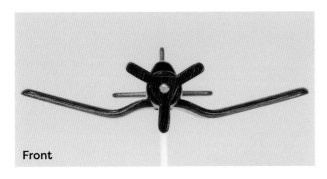
Front

Back

Side

Top

## TEMPLATES

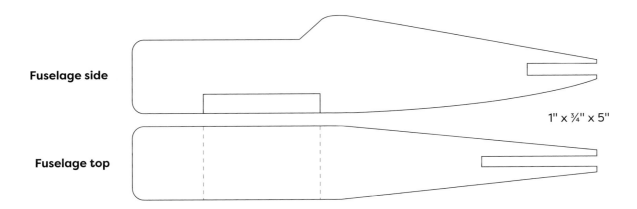

**Fuselage side**

**Fuselage top**

1" × ¾" × 5"

**Wing top**

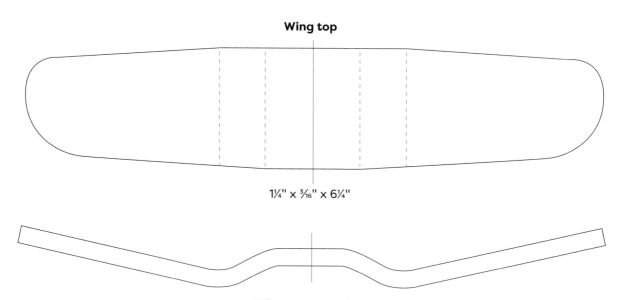

1¼" × ³⁄₁₆" × 6¼"

**Wing cross section
and bending jig template**

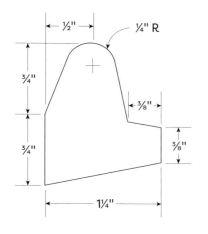

**Vertical stabilizer**

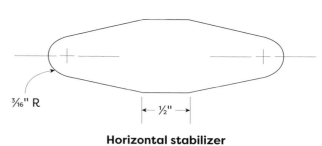

**Horizontal stabilizer**

# FRONT WING

The F4U Corsair wing has an unusual "W" shape, originally designed to fold and fit into the tight confines of an aircraft carrier. To make these wings strong enough to be played with and dropped on occasion, laminate them from thin veneers. This is also a good option for the vertical stabilizer and even the horizontal stabilizer, as well as the propeller.

**1** First, make the veneer press. Cut a length of wood at least 8 in. long by at least 1½ in. thick from 2 x 4 softwood lumber. Mark out the contour using the template. The complex "W" shape is best made with two cuts to create even pressure throughout the wing shape. Saw down the middle first to rough out the shape.

**2** Saw to the lines. Do this as carefully as possible. If you have any large ripples, sand or file the worst of them off; otherwise sanding is not necessary.

**3** Cut veneer strips about 2 in. wide by 8 in. long. You may need to wet the veneer to keep it from splitting when cutting. The combined thickness is about ³⁄₁₆ in. Veneer thickness varies, so cut strips and combine them to add up to ³⁄₁₆ in., give or take ¹⁄₃₂ in. The top three and bottom one or two veneers should have their grain oriented lengthwise. In between, the layers should alternate grain direction.

**4** Wipe both sides of each veneer with a wet (not dripping) cloth and clamp in place without glue. Let dry in this position, which will take a few hours.

**5** Cut thin strips of foam, such as laminate flooring underlay, to act as cushions to spread the pressure evenly so the glue lines remain closed over the whole wing. Place the cushioning on the bottom and top of the press. Put each veneer down in order, spreading glue evenly on each one. Use a good veneering glue, such as Titebond III. Align the veneers and the press; clamp the assembly.

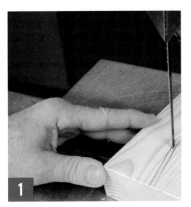
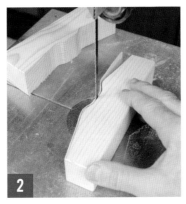

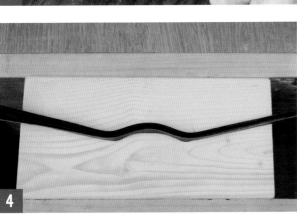

**6** After the glue is thoroughly dry (best to leave overnight to reduce the tendency to straighten slightly), mark out the wing contour with the template or by measurement. Saw and sand to the lines.

**7** Disc-sand the straight center sections on the front and back edges so they are straight and parallel. Holding the wing tips equal distance from the sander will help keep these surfaces correct. If desired, shape the wings into an approximation of an airfoil while still leaving the edges rounded and smooth. Rough it out with a disc sander or rasp, then finish it with a fine small file and sandpaper. Leave the wing shape squared off between the centering lines.

## REAR WING & TAIL (HORIZONTAL & VERTICAL STABILIZERS)

**1** Choose a wood type. The strongest option is to make thin plywood using the veneer you used for the wing. Close-grained solid ⅛ in.-thick hardwood is another option, though it has a slight risk of breaking along a grain line; orient the grain lengthwise for the horizontal stabilizer and vertically for the vertical stabilizer. A compromise is ⅛ in. Baltic birch plywood; it has good strength in all directions and is readily available. However, you may need to buy much more than you need, and it can splinter along the cut edges. Whichever you choose, it will need to fit the dadoes cut using the ⅛ in.-thick tablesaw blade, so you may want to do a test cut to make sure the wood fits in the dado.

**2** Glue the veneer, if that is your choice. To make both parts, clamp 3 in. x 3 in. veneer pieces between two flat blocks of wood. Try to have the thickness end up the same size as the dado cut, or just over (¹⁄₆₄ in. to ¹⁄₃₂ in.). The laminated parts can be sanded slightly thinner if needed to fit the dado.

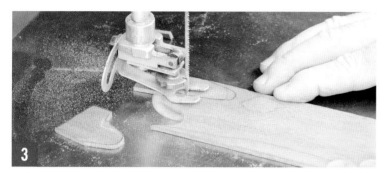

**3** **Mark out the contour. Saw out the** parts, then file and sand the outside contour to the lines. The vertical stabilizer is best cut about ⅛ in. oversize on the bottom edge and trimmed flush later. Sand the stabilizers, leaving the areas that will be glue surfaces, but breaking exposed sharp edges.

# FUSELAGE

**1** **Cut the block to rough size, then lay** out the templates. Have the tail end of the template at or very near one end of the wood. This will make it easier to cut the dadoes for the stabilizers. For very dark wood, consider marking the outlines on masking tape.

**2** **The vertical stabilizer dado is best** cut on the tablesaw, although the bandsaw can be used with careful layout and sawing. Clamp the fuselage block to the miter gauge. Set the blade to 1¼ in. deep and place the fuselage block vertically square to the table. The dado should be centered on the fuselage.

**3** **Check the wing dado width. The** dado should be a tiny bit smaller (about 1/32 in.) than the wing. It is easier to fit the wing to the dado than it is to re-cut the dado later.

**4** **Cut the wing dado using the tablesaw.** Set the saw blade to 3/16 in. depth. Use the miter gauge to make a careful cut at each end of the dado to define the length, then make repeated passes until the entire dado is roughed out.

**5** Saw the top slope from the cockpit on back, then file and sand smooth. This surface is much easier to smooth now than after the vertical stabilizer is glued in place.

**6** Fit the vertical stabilizer into the slot. File and sand until the front edge fits tightly into the slot top and bottom. Glue the vertical stabilizer in place. Clamp the sides of the fuselage onto the vertical stabilizer.

**7** Using the same setup as used for the vertical stabilizer dado, saw the horizontal stabilizer dado to a depth of ¾ in.

**8** Partially saw the side profile. Leave the parts attached so the top profile can be sawn.

**9** Mark out the top profile. Use the template or measurements. For safety and accuracy, use a clamp to hold the small part. Taper the sides on the back inch or so.

**10** Finish the side profile cuts.

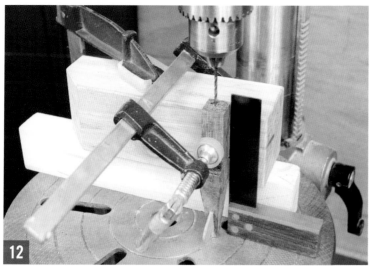

**11** Put the fuselage in your bench vise, square end up. Find the center of the square, make a small awl mark, and draw the circle with a compass or dividers. This is the round shape of the engine cowling.

**12** Next is the propeller screw hole. For a #4 screw, usually a $5/64$ in. drill bit works best. For a brass screw in hard wood (see page 118), you may have to use a $3/32$ in. bit. Clamp the fuselage to a large square block of wood and check with a square. Alternatively, you could also swivel the drill press table to 90°.

**13** Round the fuselage nose. It is round from the cockpit forward; from the cockpit back, the fuselage becomes more egg-shaped, with the smaller end being on top.

**14** Shape the cockpit area. Draw estimation lines that start about ¼ in. apart at the top of the windshield and angle down to the wider sides at the bottom of the windshield. Start filing the sloped sides flat, then round them over. Take your time to get a good transition from windshield to rounded fuselage; alternate filing the windshield and the rounded fuselage.

**15** Shape the bottom of the fuselage. Round over the corners to ⅛ in. radius at the windshield area and ¹⁄₁₆ in. radius at the tail. The fuselage, wing, and stabilizer should also be sanded now.

**16** Glue the horizontal stabilizer in place. It should be a snug fit, but if needed, clamp to close any gap. Remove squeeze-out when the glue is rubbery. When the glue is dry, sand the horizontal stabilizer flush with the fuselage end. Finish-sand the area.

**17** Dry-fit the wing into the fuselage dado. You will likely need to sand the wing front or back to get the width to exactly match. If you use a disc sander, be gentle and make sure the wing is parallel to the disc. Center the wing side to side and make small pencil marks on the wing to mark the location. If needed, file the wing top flat in the center glue area. Do this carefully, using slow small cuts with pressure right over the filing area.

**18** Apply glue to the dado and clamp the wing into place. Remove excess glue and finish-sand the plane.

# PROPELLER

**1** **Cut three to five pieces of veneer** at least 2 by 2 in. square. The total thickness should be between ³⁄₃₂ and ⅛ in. thick; a little bulkier than exact scale would have it. Laminate them, alternating the grain direction. Use sturdy clamping blocks, and some plastic or paper to prevent adhering to the blocks.

**2** **When the glue dries, sand the surfaces** smooth, then use the template to mark out the propeller contour. Mark the center with an awl. Drill the center hole. A #4 brass screw as shown should work with a ⅛ in. hole.

**3** **Use a coping saw, scroll saw, or a** bandsaw with a narrow blade to cut out the propeller. Remove the saw marks with a very small file, or sand to smooth the cut edges.

## FINISHING

See notes on finishing, page 23.

When the finish is dry, rub a bit of paraffin wax on the inside surface of the propeller, and the front of the cowling, so it spins freely. Screw the propeller to the plane, and it is ready to fly.

# F-16 FIGHTER JET

The F-16 fighter jet was developed in 1976 for the United States Air Force. If you have ever admired the Thunderbirds' flying maneuvers, you are watching F-16s at work. These nimble supersonic jets are used in the air forces of more than 20 countries. The toy as pictured requires quite a bit of hand-shaping to round and smooth all the surfaces. However, you can leave the corners only slightly rounded.

## CUT LIST

| NO. REQ'D | PART NAME | MATERIAL | T" | W" | L" | NOTES |
|---|---|---|---|---|---|---|
| 1 | Center layer, horizontal stabilizers (rear wings) | Hardwood | ⅛ | 1½ | 2½ | Note grain direction. See instructions. |
| 1 | Center layer, wings | Hardwood | ⅛ | 3 | 4 | Note grain direction. See instructions. |
| 1 | Center layer, nose | Hardwood | ⅛ | ¾ | 1⅝ | Note grain direction. See instructions. |
| 1 | Vertical stabilizer (tail) | Hardwood | ⅛ | 1¾ | 3¼ | Note grain direction. See instructions. |
| 1 | Fuselage, upper section | Hardwood | ⅜ | 1 | 5⅞ | Rough-cut about 12 in. long if possible. See instructions. |
| 1 | Fuselage, lower section | Hardwood | 5/16 | ¾ | 6⅜ | Rough-cut about 12 in. long if possible. See instructions. |
| 1 | Canopy | ⅜ in. dowel | | | 1⅝ | Rough-cut longer if possible. See instructions. |

*Note: Dimensions are finished sizes. Most parts should be rough-cut oversize. See instructions.*

## ASSEMBLY GUIDE

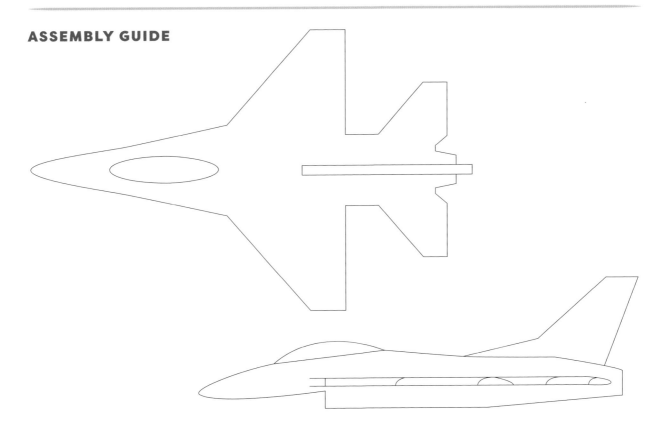

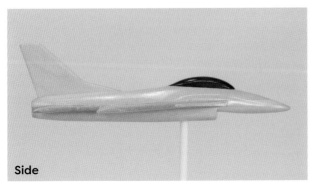

Side

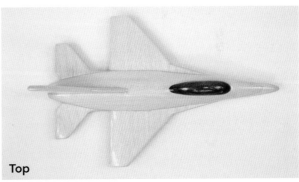

Top

Front

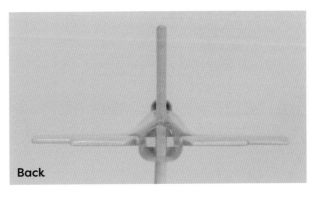

Back

## TEMPLATES
*Fuselage*

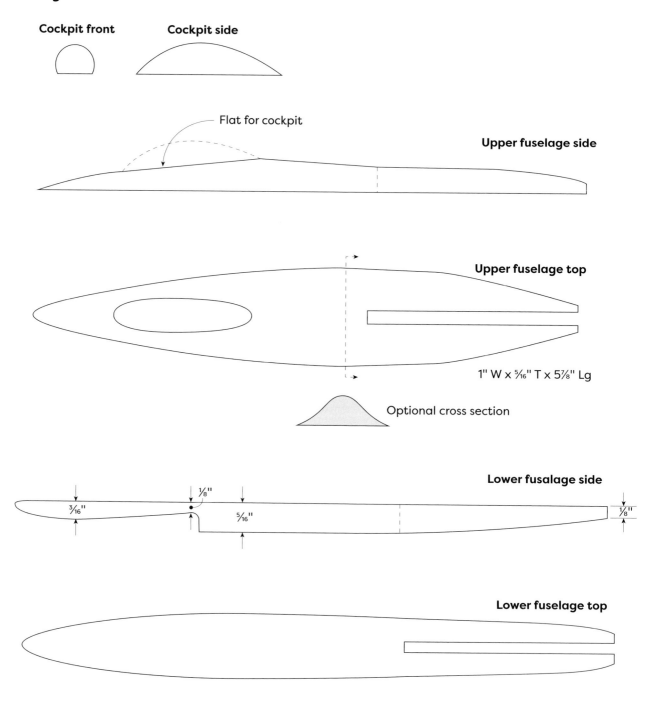

**Cockpit front**

**Cockpit side**

Flat for cockpit

**Upper fuselage side**

**Upper fuselage top**

1" W x ⁵⁄₁₆" T x 5⅞" Lg

Optional cross section

**Lower fusalage side**

³⁄₁₆"    ⅛"    ⁵⁄₁₆"    ⅛"

**Lower fuselage top**

## TEMPLATES
### Wings & Tail

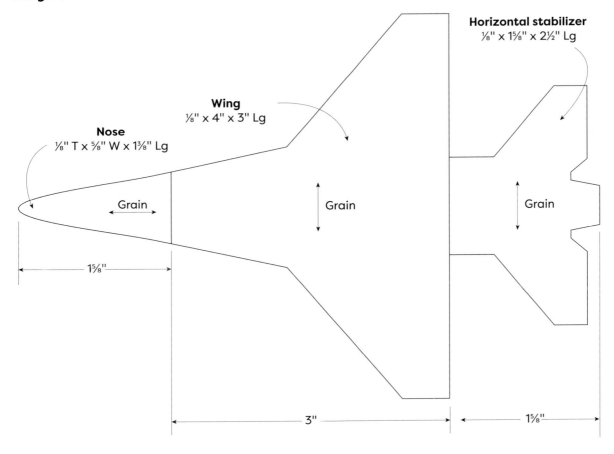

**Horizontal stabilizer**
⅛" x 1⅝" x 2½" Lg

**Wing**
⅛" x 4" x 3" Lg

**Nose**
⅛" T x ⅝" W x 1⅜" Lg

Grain

Grain

Grain

1⅝"

3"

1⅝"

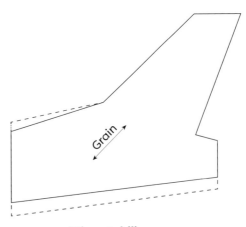

Grain

**Wing stabilizer**
⅛" T x 2⅛" W (rough) x 2¼" Lg

# CENTER LAYER: WINGS & HORIZONTAL STABILIZERS

This three-piece layer is made from ⅛ in.-thick hardwood, with the grain direction running as indicated on the templates. Hardwood strips 3 in. wide by ⅛ in. thick are readily available. The join lines are marked on the template.

**1** Mark the contours using the templates. Place join lines on the straight-jointed edges of the wood. You may want to mark out and cut the vertical stabilizer at this time also; it is likely made from the same piece of wood. Use the template, which is ⅛ in. oversize for now, so it will protrude below the fuselage, to be trimmed after assembly. It has the grain running on an angle, following the angle of the stabilizer itself. Saw the contours.

# FUSELAGE

## ROUGH SHAPING OF BOTH SECTIONS

**1** Rough out the wood blanks so they are at least 12 in. long by ⅜ in. thick for now. The upper section should be at least 1 in. wide. The lower section will need to be at least ¾ in. wide. The 12 in. length allows safe machining, and gives some extra stock so you can grip either end in a vise; this will make shaping and rounding much easier. Mark out the top and side contours of each section.

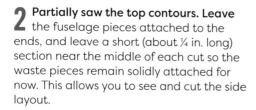

**2** Partially saw the top contours. Leave the fuselage pieces attached to the ends, and leave a short (about ¼ in. long) section near the middle of each cut so the waste pieces remain solidly attached for now. This allows you to see and cut the side layout.

**3** Saw the side contours. Leave the extra at the ends solidly attached. Use a clamp to hold these narrow parts on edge for sawing. This is safer, and makes it easier to hold them at 90° to the table.

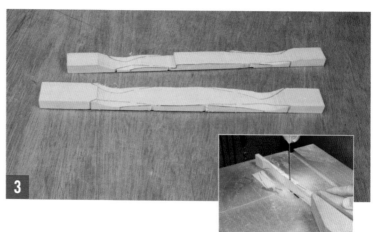

**4** **Finish the side cuts. This will complete** the shape of the sides.

## UPPER SECTION REFINEMENT

**1** **Mark out the canopy flat on the** fuselage top. This is so it stays reasonably flat while rounding the rest of the fuselage. The flat starts about ¾ in. from the front, and is about 1¾ in. long by ⅜ in. wide. Later, it can be accurately sized a bit smaller.

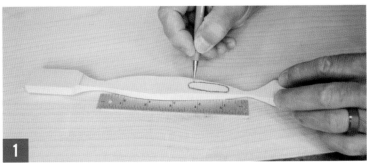

**2** **Re-mark the fuselage profile. Use the** template to draw the lines that will guide the final shaping. File or sand to the lines.

**3** **Rough out the shape of the back half.** Form the rough triangular shape, leaving a flat (about ⅛ in. wide) at the top, and a very small (¹⁄₃₂ in.) flat along the bottom edges.

**4** **Use a smooth file or coarse sandpaper** to round over the top of the triangular cross sectional area.

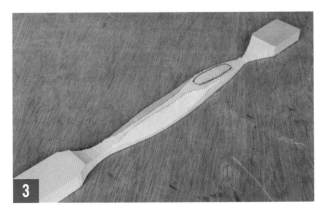

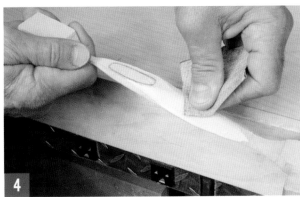

**5** **Round over the top of the nose and** cockpit area. Leave the oval flat where the cockpit will attach. Blend this more vertical rounding below the canopy with the flatter contour of the fuselage behind the canopy. Saw off the surplus. The layout lines should still appear on the flat side, but can be re-marked as needed.

**6** **Flatten the canopy mount flat section** with a small sanding board. Place the fuselage on a flat surface and rest a straightedge on the cockpit flat. It should be parallel to the flat surface. Adjust as needed.

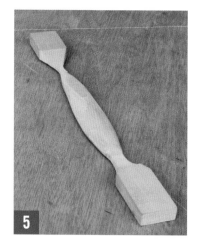

## LOWER SECTION REFINEMENT

**1** **As with the upper section, re-mark** the profile, then file or sand to the lines. The thicker section of the fuselage has larger rounds, between ⅛ and ³⁄₁₆ in. radius. This is just for appearance, so the important thing is to keep the part symmetrical side to side.

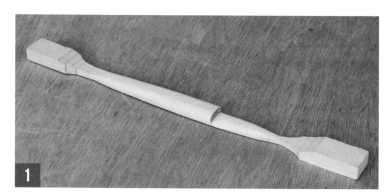

## FINISH-SANDING FOR BOTH

**1** **On both pieces, finish-sand all along** the edges that will contact the wing surfaces. These areas are much more difficult to sand after assembly. Then cut the surplus off, and leave these cut ends unsanded front and back. They are smoothed and rounded after assembly.

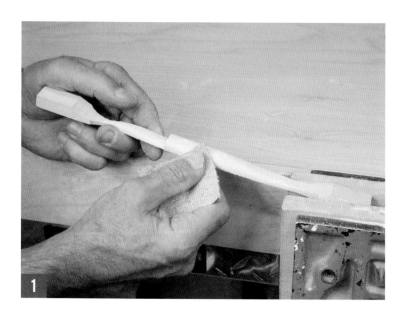

# COCKPIT CANOPY

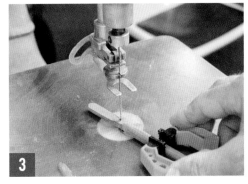

**1** Cut a 3 in. or longer piece of ⅜ in. dowel. Use a contrasting wood dowel if possible. Mark out the bottom flat that will be glued to the fuselage. Measure down ¼ in. on the end of the dowel, then carry the lines down the sides for about 2 in.

**2** Cut the flat with a saw, or sand it flat on a disc sander. If sawing, use a clamp to keep the dowel from spinning. Sand the sawn surface flat and smooth. A sanding board works well for this.

**3** Use a template, or just sketch by eye, the approximate teardrop shape on the bottom. Partially saw or file the oval shape. If using a saw, hold the dowel with a clamp to keep the dowel from spinning. Keep the canopy attached to the dowel by a thin (³⁄₁₆ in. wide) strip. This provides a handle to use when doing the final shaping.

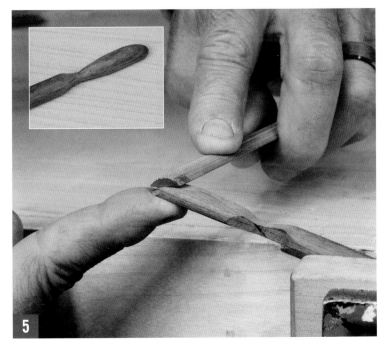

**4** Mark out the side profile. Use the small template, or draw it freehand and estimate a smooth arc. Either way it won't be perfect on the curved dowel, but you only need the rough idea. Cut the side contour. Use a scroll saw, coping saw or even a disc sander. It is still best to keep the canopy attached to the dowel.

**5** Smooth the contours. Carefully use a small file or medium sandpaper to smooth the saw marks, front and back. Round all sharp edges. The canopy should be smoothly rounded in all directions and symmetrical side to side.

**6** Saw the nearly finished cockpit from the dowel. Smooth the last cut to blend in with the other curves. Sand the cut surfaces smooth and rounded. Blend the curves. The curves should come almost to a sharp edge, especially at the back where it will blend into the fuselage contours.

# CANOPY TO FUSELAGE ASSEMBLY

**1** Mark the canopy outline on the fuselage. Locate it in line with the fuselage and centered side to side. Check by eye, then draw a thin light pencil line on the fuselage, tracing the outline. It's best if the line is about 1/32 in. away from the canopy and light enough to be easily removed later.

**2** Finish rounding the fuselage, if needed. Likely the rough flat is larger than the canopy size. If so, file or sand the fuselage to reduce the flat to within about 1/32 in. of the line.

**3** When the canopy sits flat on the fuselage, carefully sand off the thin light pencil line, then glue it in place. Press it down firmly to squeeze out any excess glue, then leave it to set until dry. Clamping is nearly impossible, and not necessary. Remove any glue squeeze-out and smooth the area around the canopy, and file or sand to blend the canopy into the fuselage contours. When it looks acceptable to you, the canopy is complete.

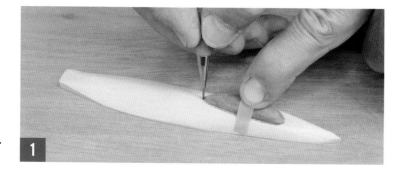

# WINGS TO UPPER FUSELAGE ASSEMBLY

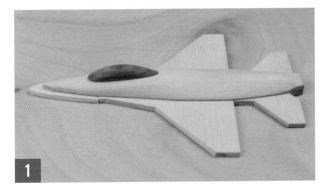

**1** **Smooth the previously cut wing parts.** Remove saw marks, and size the three parts to the lines. Dry-fit the parts. The tail end should line up flush, but the nose of the ⅛ in.-thick section will protrude. Shape and smooth that after assembly.

**2** **Glue the fuselage to the two wing** sections. Center the parts carefully side to side, and have the tail ends flush. Align the parts by eye side to side. The rear engine exhaust (nozzle) parts should align closely, so start there. Carefully remove glue squeeze-out while the glue is still rubbery.

**3** **Glue the ⅛ in.-thick nose to the** fuselage assembly. Again, center it side to side. It will protrude about 3⁄16 to ¼ in. past the nose of the fuselage.

# FUSELAGE, LOWER SECTION

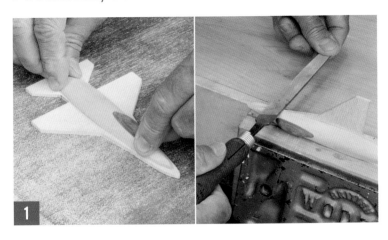

**1** **Use a sanding board to get the** bottom surface flat in preparation for attaching the lower section of the fuselage. Just at the front of the canopy, make the ⅛ in.-thick nose piece flush with the fuselage sides. You just need a small section, maybe ½ in. or so, to allow you to align the front of the fuselage bottom at the jet intake area.

**2** Glue the lower section to the fuselage assembly. Be careful to align the parts at the front and rear of the jet. Clamp the ends first to ensure alignment, then clamp the center areas. Before the glue is completely hard, remove any squeeze-out.

**3** Mark out the approximate nose profile. Do this by eye, copying the general profile from the drawings.

**4** File the nose to smooth the different layers. This is mostly done by eye, comparing the jet to the profile drawings. You could use a disc sander, but still do the last bit by hand. When smoothing the sides of the nose cone, keep the contour as side-to-side symmetrical as possible.

**5** Round the corners to form the final cone shape. The cross section should be mostly round near the tip, transitioning to the slightly less rounded shape just in front of the intake scoop under the canopy. Don't do the final sanding until the vertical dado is cut.

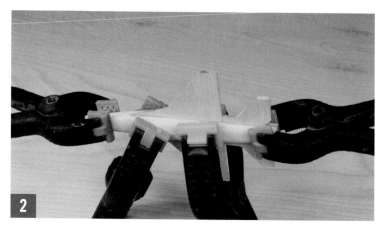

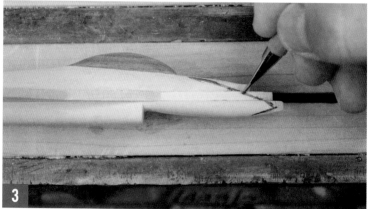

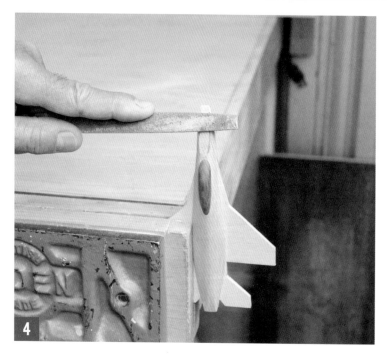

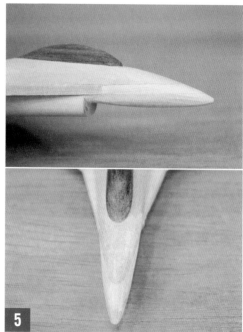

# CONCAVE SHAPING OF THE FUSELAGE (OPTIONAL)

**PROJECT NOTES**

The cross section of the fuselage is bell-shaped behind the cockpit. The edge of the fuselage can be thinned to blend into the wing. However, it is time-consuming and makes only a slight difference in appearance.

**1** **If desired, carefully file a groove from** the back of the cockpit to the front of the horizontal stabilizer, about halfway up the fuselage side. Widen this groove a bit at a time, being careful not to touch the wings, but going almost to the wings. Some tape on the wings gives a little protection for those surfaces. Use very short, controlled movements with the file.

**2** **When the rough contour suits you,** leave it for now. Sand it smooth after the wing shaping is finished.

# VERTICAL STABILIZER DADO

**1** **Mark out the top center of the jet** exhaust nozzle, where the vertical stabilizer will be installed. The dado layout is ⅛ in. wide. You could very carefully make this cut using a bandsaw, but the tablesaw is more accurate. Use two equal-thickness spacers, at least ⅜ in. thick, to allow you to clamp the jet to the miter gauge. The wings will rest against these spacers, with the fuselage between. Check that the jet is vertical by lining up the tip of the nose with the pencil layout at the tail end.

**2** Set the blade to the 2 ¼ in. depth. Have the fuselage centered to the blade side to side, and standing up square to the table. Cut the dado.

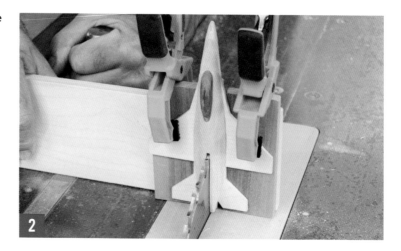

## WING AIRFOIL SHAPING (OPTIONAL)

**1** This step is not required at all, so feel free to just round over all the corners and sharp edges. File or sand the surfaces of the wings to hint at the airfoil shape. Leave the trailing edge rounded somewhat, even though an accurate model would have it very sharp.

## VERTICAL STABILIZER ASSEMBLY

**1** Fit the vertical stabilizer to the fuselage. You may need to thin the stabilizer slightly by sanding. Check that the front fits tightly against the end of the dado, while the back is approximately centered vertically in the fuselage. To have it fit nicely front and back, carefully adjust the angle at the front of the vertical stabilizer.

**2** Mark the vertical stabilizer outline. While the stabilizer is temporarily in place in the dado, do a final marking. Remove the stabilizer to saw or sand it within ⅟₃₂ in. of the lines.

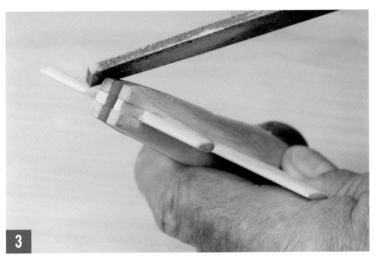

**3** **Rough out the round exhaust end.** Some of this shaping is easier to do before the stabilizer is glued in, so you may want to start the rounding now.

**4** **Spread glue in the dado using a** toothpick; slide the stabilizer into place. Make sure it is all the way in, butted against the end the dado. When the glue is dry, file or sand the bottom and back surfaces flush with the fuselage and jet exhaust nozzle.

**5** **Round out the exhaust nozzle. This** doesn't have to be a perfect circle, but should be somewhat rounded.

# FINISHING

For finishing information, please see page 23.

# HELICOPTER

This toy is modeled after the Bell UH-1. As one of the best known and widely flown helicopters, the small die-cast version has been popular for more than 50 years. This toy is made from three strips of wood, with real rotating main and tail rotors. Whether you imagine your finished toy to be a news chopper, an aerial firefighter, or a sight-seeing tour guide, get ready for some fun!

## CUT LIST

| NO. REQ'D | PART NAME | MATERIAL | T" | W" | L" | NOTES |
|---|---|---|---|---|---|---|
| 3 | Fuselage sides and center | Hardwood to match | ½ | 1⅛ | 5 | Cut 6 in. rough length. See instructions for details. |
| 1 | Tail rotor pylon | Hardwood | ⅛ | ½ | 1⅜ | Note grain direction. |
| 1 | Tail rotor spacer | Hardwood | ⅛ | ½ | ½ | |
| 1 | Tailplane (optional) | Hardwood | ⅛ | ¼ | 1 | |
| 1 | Tail rotor | Hardwood or laminated hardwood | ⅛ | ⁵⁄₁₆ | 1¼ | |
| 1 | Main rotor | Hardwood or laminated hardwood | ⅛ | ⅝ | 5½ | May be ½ in. longer or shorter; see instructions. |
| 2 | Skid struts | Baltic birch plywood | ⅛ | ½ | 1½ | See instructions for rough-cut size. |
| 2 | Skids | ⅛ in. dia. dowel | | | 1⅝ | |
| 1 | Nozzle | ¼ in. dowel to fit | | | ½ | See instructions for rough-cut size. |
| 1 | Mast | ⅜ in. dowel to fit | | | 1 | See instructions for rough-cut size. |

*Note: Dimensions are finished sizes. Most parts should be rough-cut oversize. See instructions.*

## ASSEMBLY GUIDE

**Side**

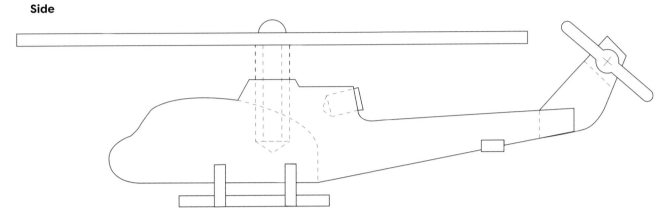

**Top**

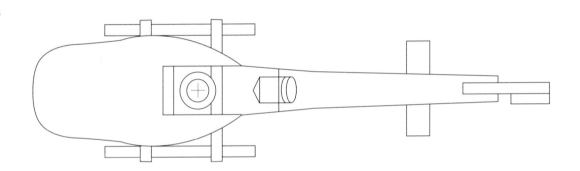

**Assembled top profile**

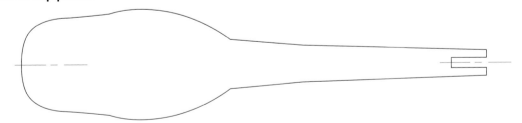

Front

Side

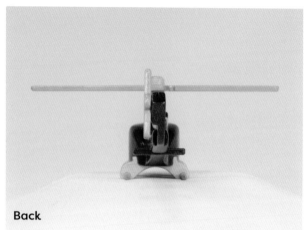

Back

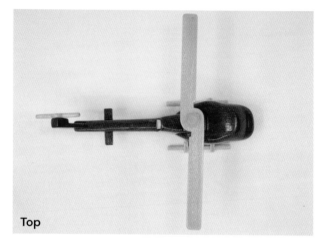

Top

## TEMPLATES

**Center top**

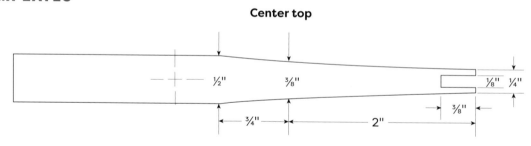

½"    ⅜"    ⅛"   ¼"

¾"    2"    ⅜"

**Center side**

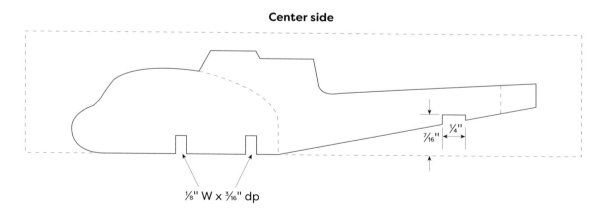

7/16"   ¼"

⅛" W x 3/16" dp

## Cockpit top

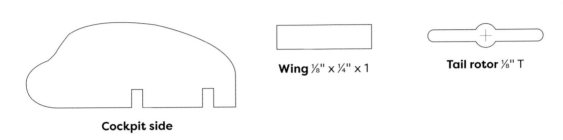

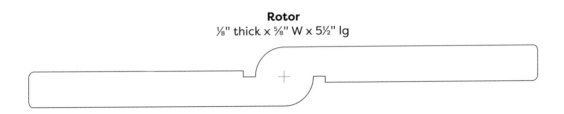

**Wing** ⅛" × ¼" × 1

**Tail rotor** ⅛" T

**Cockpit side**

## Rotor
⅛" thick × ⅝" W × 5½" lg

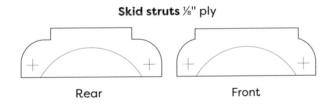

## Skid struts ⅛" ply

Rear

Front

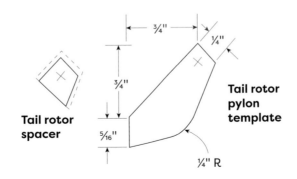

**Tail rotor spacer**

**Tail rotor pylon template**

¾"

¼"

¾"

5⁄16"

¼" R

# FUSELAGE

**1** **The fuselage is made from three pieces** of ½ in.-thick wood. This allows the center strip to have a different profile than the sides. Match the grain and color so the glue lines are less obvious; ideally from the same piece of wood. You will need a small ⅛ in.-thick piece of the same wood for the tail rotor pylon. Cut the strips at least 1 in. longer than finished length. Temporarily spot-glue the strips together at the very ends of the boards.

**2** **Draw a reference line ½ in. from the** front. Use a square to continue this line around the block's top and sides (see page 28). This line will be used to locate top and side profiles. Draw a centerline. This will help locate the template and the tail rotor pylon dado.

**3** **Mark a reference line at the tail end,** as you did at the front. This should be about 5 in. from the front line. Use a template to trace the top profile. Mark out the rotor mast hole location with an awl. Trace (or measure out) the dado locations. If adding a rear wing, mark that dado also.

**4** **Mark the tail rotor pylon dado depth** at ⅜ in., measured from the tail end reference line.

**PROJECT NOTES**

The skid assembly is detailed and requires some careful work. You may want to use a simpler option, which is to drill four holes for small dowel feet. These could be made from ⅛ or 3/16 in. dowel. In this case, do not cut the skid dados. Omit step 6 below.

**5**

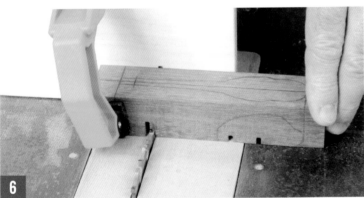

**6**

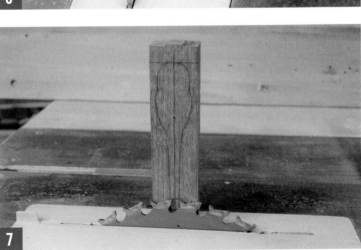

**7**

**5** Trace the cockpit side profile on both sides.

**6** Cut the dados for the skids, and for the optional rear wing, if desired.

**7** Set the saw depth for the tail rotor pylon dado. This will be the ⅜ in. dado depth plus the excess wood still on the block (about ½ in. as shown). Hold the wood against the blade and adjust the depth to the line. This dimension is not critical, but should be within 1/16 in. of the desired ⅜ in. final depth.

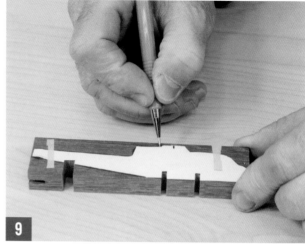

**8** Clamp the fuselage block to the miter gauge. Check for square and alignment to the centerline. This will be centered side to side. Clamp the fuselage to the miter gauge, square to the table, and make the cut for the tail rotor pylon.

**9** Trim the ends so the pieces come apart. Put the side strips away for the moment. Mark the side profile on the center strip. Use the template. If you didn't mark out the hole on top for the rotor mast earlier, do so now.

**10** Drill the rotor mast hole. Hole size and location need to be quite accurate, so drill a sample hole first (see page 19). Drill ½ to ⅝ in. deep.

**11** Cut the cabin area profile, but leave about ½ in. uncut in the tail boom so you can still see the cutting lines on the top contour lines on the tail boom area.

**12** Saw the top contour of the tail boom. It needs to be slender to keep it as light as possible so the toy doesn't tip back on the skids when complete. Use a clamp both for safety and to keep the fuselage vertical.

**13** Complete the side contour cuts.

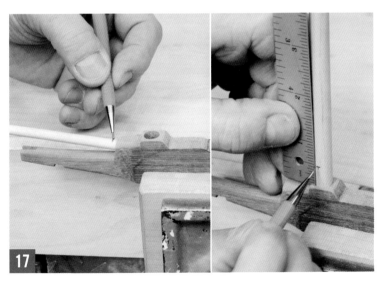

**14** **Mark out the cabin side outlines.** You don't want to file or sand in these areas because they will be glue joint surfaces. File and sand to remove saw marks. Check by eye that the boom is symmetrical and centered.

**15** **Round over the tail boom edges. On** the top, rounds are about ⅛ in. radius at the front and slightly less at the rear. On the bottom, rounds are smaller, about 1/16 in. radius. Round over the cabin's top corners slightly.

**16** **Drill the exhaust nozzle hole** approximately ⅜ in. deep. Center the hole in the small exhaust surface side to side and top to bottom. Select a bit that matches the size of your ¼ in. dowel (see page 19). The wood is held in a parallel clamp, which is itself clamped to the table. This makes it easier to adjust the angle so the drill appears to be at 90° to the small face of the engine exhaust.

**17** **Mark the length of the ¼ in. nozzle** dowel. It should protrude ⅛ in. out the hole when assembled. Mark the length of the mast dowel. It should protrude 7/16 in.

**18** Finish-sand to smooth the sides and ends of the dowels, if needed. Finish-sand the areas around the dowel holes. This is much easier now than it is after the dowels are in place. Put glue sparingly in the holes (to reduce squeeze-out), and then push or tap in the short dowels.

**19** Use an awl to mark center of the top dowel for the rotor pivot pin (factory axle pin), which is usually 7/32 in. diameter. If you would rather use a wood screw, drill to fit the screw. Use the same setup used to drill the mast dowel hole. Drill about 1 in. deep.

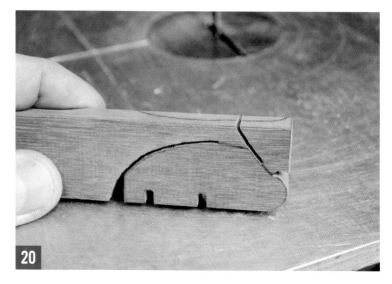

**20** Partially saw the side profile of the cockpit sides to shape. Leave a small section so that you can still see the contour lines on the top, and leave them attached to the larger piece until the top profile is cut.

**21** Saw the top profiles to the lines. This is bit easier to hold straight up if the part is held in a clamp.

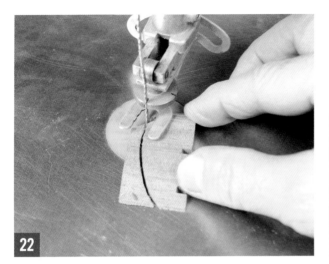

**22** Finish sawing the side profiles. Use a scroll saw or coping saw for these small parts.

**23** File and sand the areas that will not be easily accessible later when the sides are glued to the center. This is mostly the top and back of the cockpit sides.

**24** Dry-clamp the three strips. Check that they sit flat, and that the sanding is complete in those areas that will be hard to reach. Use ⅛ in. plywood strips or dowels to align the dadoes. Unclamp and apply glue. Align again with the strips or dowels, but remove after clamping so they don't get stuck. Clamping the small edge works best using clamps with swivel pads.

**25** Shape the rounded surfaces. Bandsaw the rough shape of the nose, then file and hand-sand. The exact sizes of the rounds are not critical, but try to keep the sides symmetrical. The nose is very rounded; the windshield somewhat less.

# TAIL ROTOR PYLON & ROTOR SPACER

**PROJECT NOTES**

These are three small parts cut from ⅛ in. thick wood. The spacer is glued to the pylon so the rotor can spin freely. This small assembly is glued into the dado at the rear of the tail boom. The tailplane, if your toy is going to have one, is fitted into the dado on the underside of the tail boom.

**1** **Mark out the parts on ⅛ in.-thick wood.** Position the tail rotor pylon so the grain is running in line with the pylon itself. Cut the parts out.

**2** **Sand the larger end of the spacer. The** other three edges are sanded after the assembly is sawn out.

**3** **Glue the spacer to the pylon. Have it** protrude about 1⁄32 in. from top and sides. When the glue is dry, file or sand the edges flush.

**4** **Test-fit the tail rotor pylon into the** dado. Sand the thickness if needed. Check and eliminate any gap at the front of the pylon where it meets the end of the dado. Leave the bottom of the outline oversize for now, then trim flush to the fuselage later.

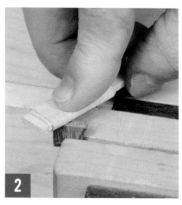

**5** Put glue into the dado using a toothpick, and a small amount of glue on the pylon sides where they fit into the dado. Press the pylon firmly into place, then clamp the sides lightly. When dry, file and sand the pylon flush. The pylon should be even with the bottom of the tail boom. Smooth the contour and round over any exposed sharp corners.

**6** Determine the pilot hole size for the wood screw you will be using (see page 118). It should be about ⅛ in. down from the top, and ⅛ in. in from the front. The drilled hole should be as deep as possible without breaking through (¹⁄₃₂ to ¹⁄₁₆ in. short); either set a stop or mark the depth with masking tape on the drill bit and drill the hole.

## SKID ASSEMBLY

**1** Cut two pieces of ⅛ in. Baltic birch plywood, at least 3 in. long (or longer) by ½ in. wide. Temporarily glue the pieces together with a small dab of glue at each end. Mark the profile of the skid struts. The center marks in the corners are for the skid dowels; they should be in from the edge at least ⅛ in. Excess will be trimmed after drilling.

**2** Tape the bottom side. Masking tape reduces plywood splintering. Drill holes for the ⅛ in. dowel skids (see page 19). Saw most of the outline, then saw the other glue end off to separate the parts.

**3** Trace the smaller outline of the rear strut. It is slightly narrower at the top because the fuselage is tapered. Trim the rear strut, leaving it slightly oversize, then check the fit on the fuselage. Sand to remove the saw marks.

**4** Glue the struts to the fuselage, with the dowels temporarily in place to help align the skids. Clamping the struts is not needed; just press firmly into place. When the glue is dry, slide the skid dowels about ⅛ in. out of position. Apply glue to the skid dowels right beside the struts, then slide them the rest of the way so the glue goes into the holes in the struts.

**5** When the glue is almost dry, carefully remove any squeeze-out with a small chisel or razor knife. When completely dry, sand to remove the excess plywood around the outside and bottom of the skid dowels. The skids will be exposed on the bottom where they contact the ground. Round any sharp corners and edges on the helicopter.

## TAILPLANE (OPTIONAL)

**1** Cut the tailplane to 1 in. long by ¼ in. wide (or to fit dado) by ⅛ in. thick. Fit the tailplane to the dado. Sand all the surfaces, but leave the corners sharp for now, especially at the dado. Be generous with a good quality glue and hold in place for a moment, or clamp if needed to close a gap.

# ROTORS

These rotors can be made from a strong close-grained wood, or a laminated wood as done for the propellers of the fighter planes (see page 131). With five to seven layers of veneer about 1 x 6 in., you will have enough for both rotors, and some to spare.

**1** Mark out the rotor outlines. Use the templates. The main rotor can be shortened to 5 in. long, which makes it a little more sturdy. Mark out the hole centers. Drill the main rotor. The center hole is ¼ in., which allows ¹⁄₃₂ in. clearance on the ⁷⁄₃₂ in. axle pin.

**2** Drill the tail rotor. Countersink the hole. A flat head screw is a bit stronger, so the rotor must be countersunk to fit the screw head. If you are using a round head screw, you can skip this step.

**3** Saw the profiles. File and sand to the lines. Remove saw marks and round the edges.

## APPLY FINISH

**1** **Finish the rotors separately from the**
**fuselage.** Slide a ⁷⁄₃₂ in. axle pin into the
rotor mast, which allows for spraying finish
on the axle pin head while keeping finish
out of the rotor mast hole. Assemble the
helicopter parts only when the finish has
thoroughly dried.

## ASSEMBLE

**1** **Screw the tail rotor into place. Shown**
is a brass-plated screw, which is stronger
than an actual brass screw. A steel wood
screw would work well also. If the wood
screw is a tiny bit too long, file, sand, or
grind the tip off. Because there is a pilot
hole, the tip is not needed.

**2** **Put glue in the hole of main rotor mast.**
Put the axle pin through the rotor and
push it into place, leaving the rotor a tiny
bit loose so it spins. Use a small spacer
(see step 4, page 21) to ensure a good
spinning fit.

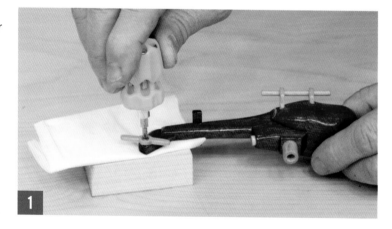

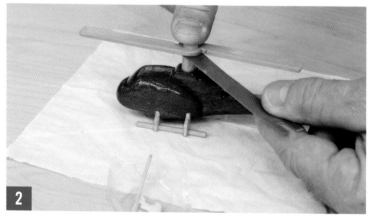

# P-51 MUSTANG FIGHTER PLANE

The P-51 Mustang is one of the most accomplished and famous WWII fighter planes. They were first produced in 1940, and were flown by some air forces into the 1980s. They are still a popular civilian racing plane. The distinctive side profile with the under-wing scoop, together with the plane's reputation and popularity, made the P-51 a top-selling die-cast toy as well. Take off from the runway and defend the skies!

## CUT LIST

| NO. REQ'D | PART NAME | MATERIAL | T" | W" | L" | NOTES |
|---|---|---|---|---|---|---|
| 4 to 8 | Wing veneers | Veneer (total thickness ³⁄₁₆ in.) | ¹⁄₆₄ to ¹⁄₃₂ | 1⅝ | 6¾ | Cut veneer oversize. Alternate grain directions. See instructions. |
| 1 | Horizontal stabilizer (rear wing) | ⅛ in. hardwood or veneer (total thickness ⅛ in.) | ⅛ | ¾ | 2½ | Cut veneer oversize. Alternate grain directions. If using solid wood, note grain direction. See instructions. |
| 1 | Vertical stabilizer (tail) | ⅛ in. hardwood or veneer (total thickness ⅛ in.) | ⅛ | 1¼ | 1⅝ | Cut veneer oversize. Alternate grain directions. If using solid wood, note grain direction. See instructions. |
| 1 | Fuselage | Hardwood | ⅝ | 1⅛ | 5⅜ | |
| 3 to 5 | Propeller veneer | Veneer (total thickness ⅛ in.) | ¹⁄₆₄ to ¹⁄₃₂ | 1½ | 1½ | Cut veneer oversize. Alternate grain directions. See instructions. |
| 1 | Air scoop | Hardwood | ¼ | ⅝ | 1⅝ | |

*Note: Dimensions are finished sizes. Most parts should be rough-cut oversize. See instructions.*

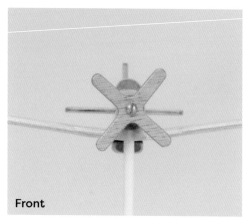

Front

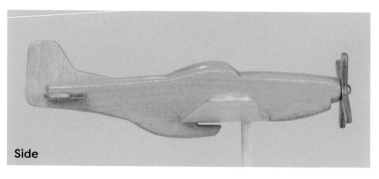

Side

Back

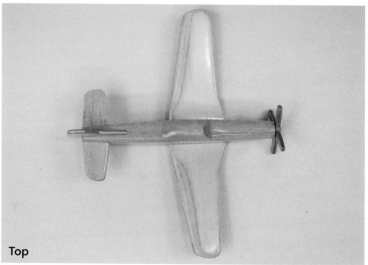

Top

## TEMPLATES

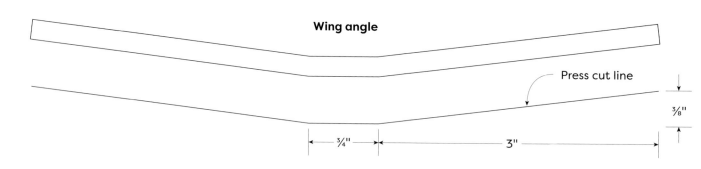

Wing angle

Press cut line

³⁄₄"

3"

³⁄₈"

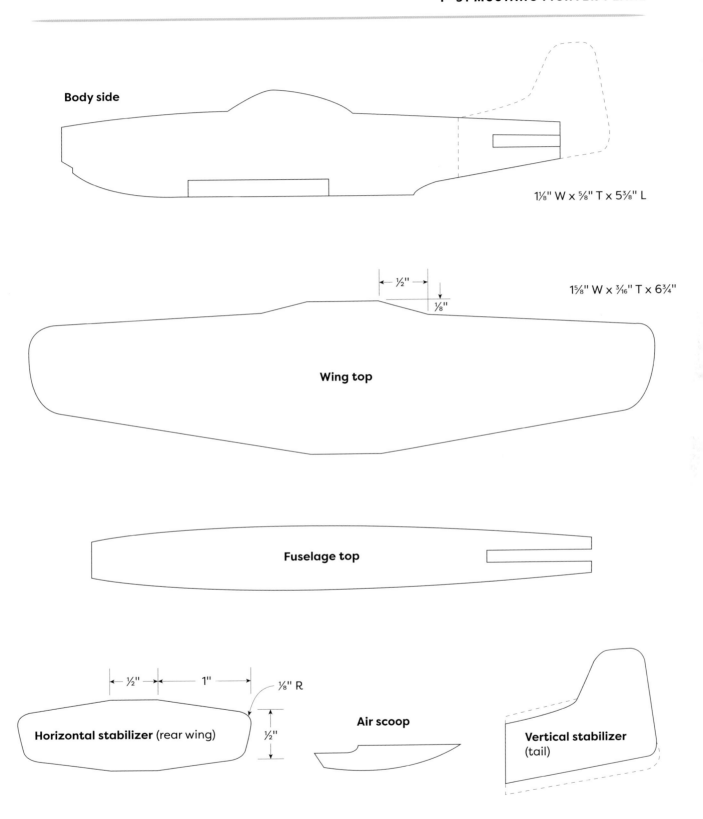

**Body side**

1⅛" W x ⅝" T x 5⅜" L

½"

⅛"

1⅝" W x ³⁄₁₆" T x 6¾"

**Wing top**

**Fuselage top**

½"     1"     ⅛" R

½"

**Horizontal stabilizer** (rear wing)

**Air scoop**

**Vertical stabilizer** (tail)

# WING

**PROJECT NOTES**

A straight wing could be made from a solid piece of hardwood for a quick and easy variation. However, a simple press to glue veneer into the shallow "V" shape is worth the extra effort.

**1** See instructions on page 131 to use the veneer press. Cut an 8 in. length of wood at least 1½ in. thick. Mark out the contour using the template and saw down the line. The veneer strips should be 2 in. wide by 8 in. long. The combined thickness should be about ³⁄₁₆ in. Here is the grain direction and order, top to bottom: top three lengthwise; alternate middle veneers; bottom one or two lengthwise. You will not need to soak these veneers before gluing.

**2** After the glue is thoroughly dry (best to leave overnight to reduce the tendency to straighten slightly) mark out the wing contour with the template or by measurement. Saw and sand to the lines.

**3** The short straight center section on the front and back edges will fit into the dado on the fuselage. These sections should be kept straight and parallel and aligned with the wing as a whole so that it sits at 90° to the fuselage dado. You can shape the wings into an approximation of an airfoil cross-section while still leaving the edges rounded and smooth.

# REAR WING & TAIL (HORIZONTAL & VERTICAL STABILIZERS)

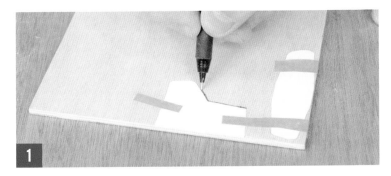

**1** See steps 1 and 2 on page 126 for selecting wood for these parts. Trace the template for the stabilizers, making the vertical stabilizer overlong on the bottom edge by about ⅛ in. or so. This part will protrude out the bottom of the fuselage and be trimmed flush after the glue is dry.

**2** Tape the underside to prevent splintering. Saw out the horizontal stabilizers. Disc-sand or hand-sand to the lines. When filing plywood, first remove sharp edges, rounding them over slightly to reduce splintering.

**3** Remove sharp edges from the stabilizers. Leave the areas that will be glue surfaces, but break the sharp edges that will be exposed. Don't bother with the airfoil shapes on either stabilizer.

# FUSELAGE

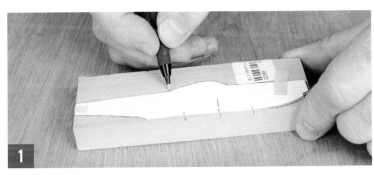

**1** The fuselage is a solid rectangular block until the dadoes are cut. Cut it to rough size. Set aside a little extra for the scoop. Ideally the scoop should be 3 or 4 in. long to make it easier to shape and handle. Mark out the fuselage side contour from the template. Have the tail end of the template at or very near one end. This will make it easier to cut the dadoes for the stabilizers.

**2** Lay out the scoop. When it is sawn to rough size, leave it attached to the longer block for the moment. This will make it easier to handle for shaping and sanding.

## DADO CUTS

**1** **Mark out all three dados. The rear ones** are centered on the fuselage, with the horizontal stabilizer dado being ¾ in. deep and the vertical stabilizer dado 1¼ in. deep. The wing dado is ³⁄₁₆ in. deep by 1¼ wide, and centered 1⅜ in. from the front.

**2** **Cut the dados for the two stabilizers** with a tablesaw. Clamp the fuselage block to the miter gauge. Set the blade to the correct depth (¾ in.) and make sure the fuselage block is vertically square to the table. Cut the dado for the vertical stabilizer in the same way.

**3** **On the fuselage, mark out the wing** dado width (see step 3, page 127). The dado should be slightly (about ¹⁄₃₂ in.) smaller than the wing width. Set the saw blade to ³⁄₁₆ in. depth. Use the miter gauge and make a cut at each end of the dado. A clamp on one end of the fuselage helps keep it stable and accurate. Make repeated passes until the entire dado is roughed out.

**4** **Partially saw the top contour of the** fuselage. Leave the sides attached, so you can still see the side contour lines.

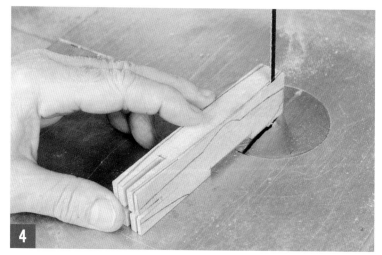

**5** Saw the side contour of the fuselage. Finish the cuts on the top contour.

**6** Mark out the propeller screw hole in the center of the fuselage and the round shape of the engine cowling. Find the center of the square shape, then draw the circle with compass or dividers.

**7** Drill the propeller screw hole (see page 129). File and sand to remove the saw marks. Slightly round the top corners at the rear of the plane where the stabilizers will be installed. Radius is about ⅟₁₆ in.

**8** Round the corners of the nose. It is round at the front cowling only, then quickly becomes more oval-shaped toward the cockpit. Leave the underside surface of the fuselage, between the wing and the vertical stabilizer, flat and straight for the air scoop. Get a good sharp transition between the cockpit and the fuselage. Alternate filing the flat windshield and the rounded fuselage.

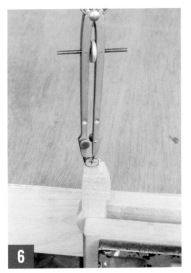

**9** Mark out the slot on the vertical stabilizer. Slide the vertical stabilizer into place, and trace out the horizontal stabilizer slot. Mark the end of the slot about ⅛ in. shorter to ensure the slot will be hidden upon assembly.

**10** Similarly, mark out the ⅛ in. notch at the back of the horizontal stabilizer. Dry-fit the horizontal stabilizer, centering it carefully. Mark out a notch ⅛ in. deep, so that the vertical stabilizer can slide into place later.

**11** Saw the slots. The slot in the vertical stabilizer can be slightly oversize, about ¹⁄₃₂ in. over width. Dry-fit the stabilizers and make sure they fit snugly. Clamping is difficult, so try to get a good fit between the stabilizers and the fuselage dados. You may need to widen the slot in the vertical stabilizer to allow it to fit well.

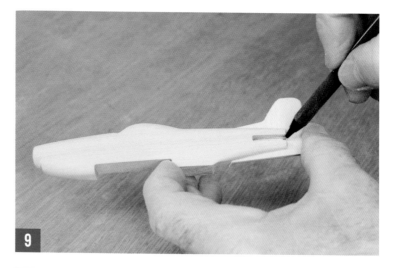

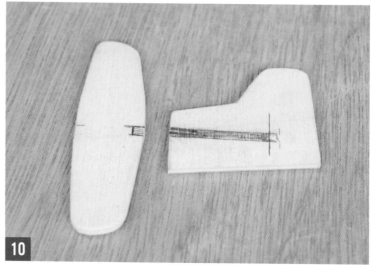

# ASSEMBLY

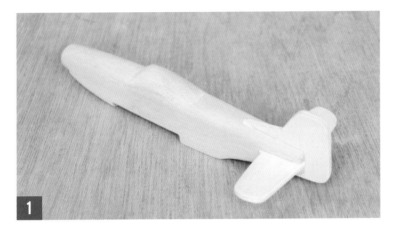

**1** **Glue the stabilizers in place. Finish-** sand the sides of the tail section before the horizontal stabilizer is attached. Be generous with the glue and glue both stabilizers in at the same time to ensure alignment all around.

**2** **When the glue is dry, smooth the** bottom surfaces flush.

**3** **Finish-sand the wing. Fit the wing into** the fuselage dado. File and sand to fit, then center it side to side. Make small pencil marks on the wing and fuselage to mark the location. Mark any adjustments to the wing contour to fit the fuselage.

**4** **When the wing has its final shape,** apply glue to the dado and clamp the wing into place. Sand the bottom surfaces flush. This is where the scoop will attach, so it needs to be straight and flat. If needed, finish-sand the bottom surface but leave the scoop glue surface untouched.

# AIR SCOOP

**1** **Retrieve the wood for the scoop that** you roughed out when you cut the fuselage. Saw to rough out the scoop, but leave it attached to the large block for now.

**2** **File and sand to round the front section** of the scoop where it will protrude under the wing. Saw the scoop from the larger block.

**3** **The bottom of the plane must be flat** to provide a good glue surface. Glue the scoop right behind the wing and match it into the profile of the fuselage. It will protrude slightly under the wing.

**4** **When the glue is dry, shape the scoop** to blend in with the fuselage. Round the sharp corners to about ⅛ in. radius.

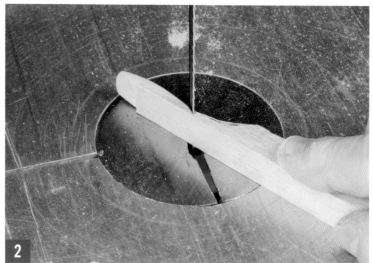

# PROPELLER

1 **The toy prop needs to be a little bulkier** than exact scale would have it, so choose veneers to make it a total of ⅛ in. thick. Cut three to five pieces of veneer to at least 2 by 2 in. square. Laminate them, alternating the grain direction.

2 **Mark out the propeller contour. Use the** template. Mark out the center with an awl.

3 **Drill the center hole and drill the four** intersecting holes that form the round where the blades intersect. The layout of the four intersecting holes allows for ¼ in. drill size, but slightly smaller (⁷⁄₃₂ in.) allows for a little sanding after.

4 **Saw the contour. Use a coping saw,** scroll saw, or a bandsaw with a narrow blade. Use a very small file or sand to smooth the cut edges. Finish-sand.

## FINISHING

See page 23 for finishing information. When the finish is dry, rub a bit of paraffin wax on the inside surface of the propeller and the front of the cowling. This helps the propeller spin freely. Screw to the plane, and it is ready to fly.

# CONVERSIONS

In this book, lengths are given in inches. If you want to convert those to metric measurements, please use the following formulas:

### FRACTIONS TO DECIMALS

$\frac{1}{8}$ = .125

$\frac{1}{4}$ = .25

$\frac{1}{2}$ = .5

$\frac{5}{8}$ = .625

$\frac{3}{4}$ = .75

### IMPERIAL TO METRIC CONVERSION

Multiply inches by 25.4 to get millimeters

Multiply inches by 2.54 to get centimeters

Multiply yards by .9144 to get meters

For example, if you wanted to convert $1\frac{1}{8}$ inches to millimeters:

1.125 in. x 25.4mm = 28.575mm

And to convert $2\frac{1}{2}$ yards to meters:

2.5 yd. x .9144m = 2.286m

# ABOUT THE AUTHOR

Les Neufeld is the father of three children, now grown. He has been making toys for them since they were toddlers, and in turn they and their friends provided years of toy-testing and feedback. Les's early training as a machinist, then woodworking and design schooling at BCIT, and eventually a master's degree in education added some useful experience as well.

He is the author of three other books: *Tremendous Toy Trucks, Making Toys that Teach,* and *Great Big Toy Trucks.*

Les and his wife Corrinne live in Kamloops, British Columbia.

# INDEX

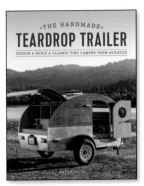
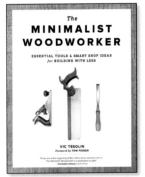

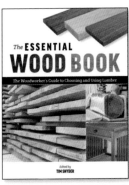

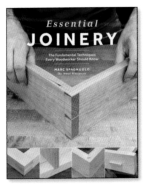

# MORE GREAT BOOKS *from*
# SPRING HOUSE PRESS

**Wooden Toy Spacecraft**
978-1-940611-83-9
$24.95 | 168 Pages

**Classic Wooden Toys**
978-1-940611-34-1
$24.95 | 176 Pages

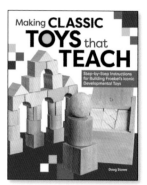

**Making Classic Toys That Teach**
978-1-940611-33-4
$24.95 | 144 Pages

**Make Your Own Cutting Boards**
978-1-940611-45-7
$22.95 | 200 Pages

**The New Bandsaw Box Book**
978-1-940611-32-7
$19.95 | 120 Pages

**Make Your Own Knife Handles**
978-1-940611-53-2
$24.95 | 168 Pages

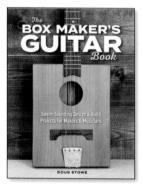

**The Box Maker's Guitar Book**
978-1-940611-64-8
$24.95 | 168 Pages

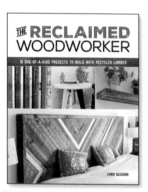

**The Reclaimed Woodworker**
978-1-940611-54-9
$24.95 | 160 Pages

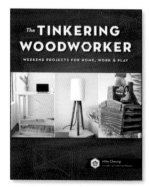

**The Tinkering Woodworker**
978-1-940611-08-2
$24.95 | 152 Pages

## SPRING HOUSE PRESS

Look for Spring House Press titles wherever books are sold or visit *www.springhousepress.com*.
For more information, call 717-569-5196 or email *info@springhousepress.com*.